WHEN THE HOLY GHOST IS COME

BY

COMMISSIONER S. L. BRENGLE, D.D., O.F.

1980 Edition
Published by
THE SALVATION ARMY
SUPPLIES AND PURCHASING DEPARTMENT
Atlanta, Georgia

First Published in 1909

ISBN: 0-86544-009-03

Printed in the United States of America

CONTENTS

PREFACE TO THE FIRST EDITION

IT is no small pleasure to me to commend this book to all who love God, and in particular to those who are labouring to serve Him in the ranks of The Salvation Army. I believe that it will prove useful in the most important way—in its bearing, that is, upon many of the practical difficulties and problems of daily life.

The writer, Colonel* Brengle, gives us not only of the fruit of an orderly and well-stored mind on the great subject before us, but—and this is the more important—he tells us of the actual work of the Holy Spirit in the lives of ordinary men and women, as he has witnessed the results of that work amidst his many labours for the salvation and holiness of the people. It is for them he writes. It is to them, living the common life, bound to others by the obligations of ordinary social intercourse, toiling at their secular occupations, and rubbing shoulders with the multitude in the market-place, that his message comes. I venture to hope that his words will make it plain to some of them that the highest intercourse with the divine is their privilege; that the special province of the Holy Ghost is to lead men into the truest devotion to God, and to the advancement of His kingdom on earth, even while they are carrying on the common avocations associated with earning their daily bread.

The only purpose of God having a practical bearing on our lives is His purpose to save men from sin and its awful consequences, and make them conform to His will in this world as in the next. The work of the Holy Spirit is to help us to achieve that purpose. Without His help we are unable to overcome the difficulties that are in the way, whether we consider them from the standpoint of the world or of the individual. If anyone could have looked at the state of the world at the time

* Later Commissioner.

of our Lord's death he would surely have regarded the work which the apostles were commissioned to attempt as the most utterly wild and impracticable enterprise that the human mind could conceive. And it was so, but for one fact. That fact was the promise of the Comforter, the Holy Spirit, to be the great Helper in the undertaking.

And equally in the work of uniting the individual soul with God's purpose that Spirit is our Helper. In the work of righteousness He is a Partner with us. In the life of faith and prayer He is our unwavering Prompter and Guide. In the submission of our wills to God and the chastening of our spirits He is the great Co-worker with us. In the bearing of burdens and the enduring of trial and sorrow He joins hands with us to lead us on. In the purifying of every power from the taint of sin He is our Sanctifier.

All this is practical. It has to do with today—with every bit of today. In fact, so far from the sphere of the Holy Spirit being limited to the pulpit or the platform, or to the inward experiences of the religious life, He is just as truly and properly concerned with the affairs of the shop and the street, the nursery and the kitchen, the chamber of suffering and the home of penury, as with preaching the gospel or healing the sick.

Now it is to lead its readers to a personal experience of all this that this book has been written. No mere intellectual assent to the truth it sets forth can satisfy its author, any more than it can benefit his readers. What he seeks, and what I join him in devoutly asking of God, is that you, dear friend, who may take this little volume into your hands, may see what an infinite privilege is yours, and may begin to act with God the Holy Ghost, and to open your whole being to Him, that He may work with you.

BRAMWELL BOOTH.

INTERNATIONAL HEADQUARTERS,
January, 1909.

WHEN THE HOLY GHOST IS COME

CHAPTER I

Who is He?

' Ye shall receive power, after that the Holy Ghost is come upon you.'

ON that last eventful evening in the upper room, just after the Passover feast, Jesus spoke to His disciples about His departure and, having commanded them to love one another, He besought them not to be troubled in heart but to hold fast their faith in Him, assuring them that, though He was to die and leave them, He was but going to the Father's many-mansioned house to prepare a place for them.

But already they were troubled; for what could this death and departure mean but the destruction of all their hopes, of all their cherished plans? Jesus had drawn them away from their fishing-boats, their places of custom and daily employment, and inspired them with high personal and patriotic ambitions, and encouraged them to believe that He was the Seed of David, the promised Messiah; and they hoped that He would cast out Pilate and his hated Roman garrison, restore the kingdom to Israel, and sit on David's throne, a King, reigning in righteousness and undisputed power and majesty for ever. And then, were they not to be His ministers of state and chief men in His kingdom?

He was their Leader, directing their labours; their Teacher, instructing their ignorance and solving their doubts and all their puzzling problems; their Defence, stilling the stormy sea and answering for them when questioned by wise and wily enemies.

They were poor and unlearned and weak. In Him was all their help; and what would they do, what could they do, without Him? They were without social standing, without financial prestige, without learning or intellectual equipment, without political or military power. He was their all, and without Him they were as helpless as little children, as defenceless as lambs in the midst of wolves. How could their poor hearts be otherwise than troubled?

But then He gave them a strange, wonderful, reassuring promise. He said: ' If ye love Me, keep My commandments. And I will pray the Father, and He shall give you another Comforter, that He may abide with you for ever ' (John xiv. 15, 16). I am going away, but Another shall come who will fill My place. He shall not go away, but abide with you for ever, and He ' shall be in you '. And later He added: ' It is expedient for you ' —that is, better for you—' that I go away: for if I go not away, the Comforter will not come ' (John xvi. 7).

Who is this other One—this Comforter? He must be some august divine Person, and not a mere influence or impersonal force; for how else could He take and fill the place of Jesus? How else could it be said that it was better to have Him than to have Jesus remaining in the flesh? He must be strong and wise, and tender and true, to take the place of the Blessed One who is to die and depart. Who is He?

John, writing in the Greek language, calls Him Paraclete, but in English we call Him Comforter. But Paraclete means more, much more than Comforter. It means ' one called in to help: an advocate, a helper '. The same word is used of Jesus in 1 John ii. 1: ' We have an Advocate (a Paraclete, a Helper) with the Father, Jesus Christ the righteous.' Just as Jesus had gone to be the disciples' Advocate, their Helper in the heavens, so this other Paraclete was to be their Advocate, their Helper on earth. He would be their Comforter when comfort was needed; but He would be more; He would be also their Teacher, Guide, Strengthener, as Jesus had been. At every point of need there would He be as an ever-present and all-wise, almighty Helper. He would meet their need with His sufficiency; their weakness with His strength; their foolishness with His wisdom; their ignorance with His knowledge; their blindness and short-sightedness with His perfect, all-embracing vision. Hallelujah! What a Comforter! Why should they be troubled?

They were weak, but He would strengthen them with might in the inner man (Eph. iii. 16). They were to give the world the words of Jesus, and teach all nations (Matt. xxviii. 19, 20); and He would teach them all things, and bring to their remembrance whatsoever Jesus had said to them (John xiv. 26).

They were to guide their converts in the right way, and He was to guide them into all truth (John xvi. 13). They were to attack hoary systems of evil, and inbred and actively intrenched sin, in every human heart; but He was to go before them, preparing the way for conquest, by convincing the world of sin, of righteousness and of judgment (John xvi. 8). They were to bear heavy burdens and face superhuman tasks, but He was to give them power (Acts i. 8). Indeed, He was to be a Comforter, a Strengthener, a Helper.

Jesus had been external to them. Often they missed Him. Sometimes He was asleep when they felt they sorely needed Him. Sometimes He was on the mountains, while they were in the valley vainly trying to cast out stubborn devils, or wearily toiling on the tumultuous, wind-tossed sea. Sometimes He was surrounded by vast crowds, and He entered into high disputes with the doctors of the law, and they had to wait till He was alone to seek explanations of His teachings. But they were never to lose this other Helper in the crowd, nor be separated for an instant from Him, for no human being, nor untoward circumstance, nor physical necessity, could ever come between Him and them for, said Jesus, ' He shall be in you'.

From the words used to declare the sayings, the doings, the offices and works of the Comforter, the Holy Spirit, we are forced to conclude that He is a divine Person. Out of the multitude of Scriptures which might be quoted, note this passage which, as nearly as is possible with human language, reveals to us His personality: ' Now there were in the church that was at Antioch certain prophets and teachers. . . . As they ministered to the Lord, and fasted, the Holy Ghost said, Separate Me Barnabas and Saul for the work whereunto I have called them. And when they had fasted and prayed, and laid their hands on them, they sent them away. So they, being sent forth by the Holy Ghost, departed into Seleucia ' (Acts xiii. 1-4).

Further on we read that they ' were forbidden of the Holy Ghost to preach the word in Asia ', and when they would have gone into Bithynia, ' the Spirit suffered them not ' (Acts xvi. 6, 7).

Again, when the messengers of Cornelius, the Roman centurion, were seeking Peter, ' the Spirit said unto him, Behold, three men seek thee. Arise therefore, and get thee down, and go with them, doubting nothing: for I have sent them ' (Acts x. 19, 20).

These are but a few of the passages of Scripture that might be quoted to establish the fact of His personality— His power to think, to will, to act, to speak; and if His personality is not made plain in these Scriptures, then it is impossible for human language to make it so.

Indeed, I am persuaded that if an intelligent heathen, who had never seen the Bible, should for the first time read the four Gospels and the Acts of the Apostles, he would say that the personality of the Holy Spirit is as clearly revealed in the Acts as is the personality of Jesus Christ in the Gospels. In truth, the Acts of the Apostles are in a large measure the acts of the Holy Spirit, and the disciples were not more certainly under the immediate direction of Jesus during the three years of His earthly ministry than they were under the direct leadership of the Spirit after Pentecost.

But, while there are those that admit His personality, yet in their loyalty to the divine Unity they deny the Trinity, and maintain that the Holy Spirit is only the Father manifesting Himself as Spirit, without any distinction in personality. But this view cannot be harmonized with certain Scriptures. While the Bible and reason plainly declare that there is but one God, yet the Scriptures as clearly reveal that there are three Persons in the Godhead—Father, Son and Holy Ghost.

The form of Paul's benediction to the Corinthians proves the doctrine:

'The grace of the Lord Jesus Christ, and the love of God, and the communion of the Holy Ghost, be with you all. Amen ' (2 Cor. xiii. 14).

Again, it is taught in the promise of Jesus, already quoted, ' And I will pray the Father, and He shall give you another Comforter . . . the Spirit of truth ' (John xiv. 16, 17). Here the three Persons of the Godhead are clearly revealed. The Son prays; the Father answers; the Spirit comes.

The Holy Spirit is ' another Comforter ', a second Comforter succeeding the first who was Jesus, and both were given by the Father.

Do you say, ' I cannot understand it '? Neither can I. Who can understand it? God does not expect us to understand it. Nor would He have us puzzle our heads and trouble our hearts in attempting to understand it or harmonize it with our knowledge of arithmetic.

Note this: it is only the *fact* that is revealed; *how* there can be three Persons in one Godhead is not revealed.

The *how* is a mystery, and is not a matter of faith at all; but the *fact* is a matter of revelation, and therefore a matter of faith. I myself am a mysterious trinity of body, mind and spirit. The fact I believe, but the *how* is not a thing to believe. It is at this point that many puzzle and perplex themselves needlessly.

In the ordinary affairs of life we grasp facts, and hold them fast, without puzzling ourselves over the *how* of things. Who can explain *how* food sustains life; *how* light reveals material objects; *how* sound conveys ideas to our minds? It is the fact we know and believe, but the *how* we pass by as a mystery unrevealed. What God has revealed, we believe. We cannot understand *how* Jesus turned water into wine; *how* He multiplied a few loaves and fishes and fed thousands; *how* He stilled the stormy sea; *how* He opened blind eyes, healed lepers and raised the dead by a word. But the facts we believe. Wireless telegraphic messages are sent over the vast wastes of ocean. That is a fact, and we believe it. But *how* they go need not be our concern. That is not something to believe.

An old servant of God has pointed out that it is the *fact* of the Trinity, and not the *manner* of it, which God has revealed and made a subject for our faith.

But while the Scriptures reveal to us the fact of the personality of the Holy Spirit (and it is a subject for our faith) to those in whom He dwells, this fact may become a matter of sacred knowledge, of blessed experience.

How else can we account for the positive and assured way in which the apostles and disciples spoke of the Holy Ghost on and after the day of Pentecost, if they did not know Him? Immediately after the fiery baptism, with its blessed filling, Peter stood before the people, and said: ' This is that which was spoken by the prophet Joel; And it shall come to pass in the last days, saith God, I will pour out of My Spirit upon all flesh ' (Acts ii. 16, 17); then he exhorted the people and assured them that if they would meet certain simple conditions they should ' receive the gift of the Holy Ghost '.   He said to

Ananias, ' Why hath Satan filled thine heart to lie to the
Holy Ghost?' (Acts v. 3). He declared to the High
Priest and Council that he and his fellow-apostles were
witnesses of the resurrection of Jesus, and added, ' So is
also the Holy Ghost, whom God hath given to them
that obey Him' (Acts v. 32). Without any apology or
explanation, or ' think so ' or ' hope so ', they speak of
being ' filled (not simply with some new, strange experience or emotion, but) with the Holy Ghost '. Certainly
they must have known Him. And if they knew Him,
may not we?

Paul says: ' Now we have received, not the spirit of
the world, but the Spirit which is of God; that we might
know the things that are freely given to us of God. Which
things also we speak, not in the words which man's
wisdom teacheth, but which the Holy Ghost teacheth '
(1 Cor. ii. 12, 13). And if we know the words, may we
not know the Teacher of the words?

John Wesley says:

> The knowledge of the Three-One God is interwoven with
> all true Christian faith, with all vital religion. I do not say
> that every real Christian can say, with the Marquis de Renty,
> ' I bear about with me continually an experimental verity, and
> a fullness of the ever-blessed Trinity. I apprehend that this
> is not the experience of " babes ", but rather " fathers in
> Christ ".' But I know not how anyone can be a Christian
> believer till he ' hath the witness in himself ', till the Spirit
> of God witnesses with his spirit that he is a child of God;
> that is, in effect, till God the Holy Ghost witnesses that God
> the Father has accepted him through the merits of God the
> Son.
>
> Not that every Christian believer adverts to this; perhaps,
> at first, not one in twenty; but, if you ask them a few questions,
> you will easily find it is implied in what they believe.

I shall never forget my joy, mingled with awe and
wonder, when this dawned upon my consciousness.
For several weeks I had been searching the Scriptures,
ransacking my heart, humbling my soul, and crying to
God almost day and night for a pure heart and the
baptism with the Holy Ghost, when one glad, sweet

day (it was January 9, 1885) this text suddenly opened to my understanding: ' If we confess our sins, He is faithful and just to forgive us our sins, and to cleanse us from all unrighteousness ' (1 John i. 9); and I was enabled to believe without any doubt that the precious Blood cleansed my heart, even mine, from all sin. Shortly after that, while reading the words of Jesus to Martha— ' I am the resurrection, and the life: he that believeth in Me, though he were dead, yet shall he live: And whosoever liveth and believeth in Me shall never die ' (John xi. 25, 26)—instantly my heart was melted like wax before fire; Jesus Christ was revealed to my spiritual consciousness, revealed in me, and my soul was filled with unutterable love. I walked in a heaven of love. Then one day, with amazement, I said to a friend: ' This is the perfect love about which the Apostle John wrote but it is beyond all I dreamed of. In it is personality. This love thinks, wills, talks with me, corrects me, instructs and teaches me.' And then I knew that God the Holy Ghost was in this love, and that this love was God, for ' God is love '.

Oh, the rapture mingled with reverential, holy fear— for it is a rapturous, yet divinely fearful thing—to be indwelt by the Holy Ghost, to be a temple of the Living God! Great heights are always opposite great depths, and from the heights of this blessed experience many have plunged into the dark depths of fanaticism. But we must not draw back from the experience through fear. All danger will be avoided by meekness and lowliness of heart; by humble, faithful service; by esteeming others better than ourselves, and in honour preferring them before ourselves; by keeping an open, teachable spirit; in a word, by looking steadily unto Jesus, to whom the Holy Spirit continually points us; for He would not have us fix our attention exclusively upon Himself and His work *in* us, but also upon the Crucified One and His work *for* us, that we may walk in the steps of Him whose Blood purchases our pardon, and makes and keeps us clean.

Great Paraclete! to Thee we cry:
O highest Gift of God most high!
O Fount of life! O Fire of love,
And sweet Anointing from above!

Our senses touch with light and fire,
Our hearts with tender love inspire;
And with endurance from on high
The weakness of our flesh supply.

Far back our enemy repel,
And let Thy peace within us dwell;
So may we, having Thee for guide,
Turn from each hurtful thing aside.

O may Thy grace on us bestow
The Father and the Son to know,
And evermore to hold confessed
Thyself of Each the Spirit blest.

' HAVE YE RECEIVED THE HOLY GHOST SINCE YE
BELIEVED? '

CHAPTER II

Preparing His House

'Ye shall receive power, after that the Holy Ghost is come upon you.'

JESUS said: ' Verily, verily, I say unto thee, Except a man be born of water and of the Spirit, he cannot enter into the kingdom of God. That which is born of the flesh is flesh; and that which is born of the Spirit is spirit ' (John iii. 5, 6). And Paul wrote to the Romans that, ' If any man have not the Spirit of Christ, he is none of His ' (viii. 9).

So it must be that every child of God, every truly converted person, has the Holy Spirit in some gracious manner and measure, else he would not be a child of God; for it is only ' as many as are led by the Spirit of God ' that ' are the sons of God ' (Rom. viii. 14).

It is the Holy Spirit who convicts us of sin, who makes us feel how good and righteous, and just and patient God is, and how guilty we are, and how unfit for Heaven, and how near to Hell. It is the Holy Spirit who leads us to true repentance and confession and amendment of life; and when our repentance is complete, and our surrender is unconditional, it is He who reasons with us, calms our fears, soothes our troubled hearts, banishes our darkness, and enables us to look to Jesus and believe on Him for the forgiveness of all our sins and the salvation of our souls. And when we yield and trust, and are accepted of the Lord, saved by grace, it is He who assures us of the Father's favour and notifies us that we are saved. ' The Spirit itself beareth witness with our spirit, that we are the children of God.' He is ' the Spirit of adoption, whereby we cry, Abba, Father ' (Rom. viii. 15, 16).

> And His that gentle voice we hear,
>   Soft as the breath of even,
> That checks each fault, that calms each fear,
>   And speaks of Heaven.

It is He who strengthens the new convert to fight against and overcome sin, and it is He who begets within him a hope of fuller righteousness through faith in Christ.

> And every virtue we possess,
>   And every victory won,
> And every thought of holiness,
>   Are His alone.

Blessed be God for this work of the Holy Spirit within the heart of every true child of His!

But, great and gracious as is this work, it is not the fiery pentecostal baptism with the Spirit which is promised; it is not the fullness of the Holy Ghost to which we are exhorted. It is only the clear dawn of the day, and not the rising of the day-star. This is only the initial work of the Spirit. It is perfect of its kind, but it is preparatory to another and fuller work, about which I wish to write.

Jesus said to His disciples concerning the Holy Spirit, that ' the world (the unsaved, unrepentant) cannot receive ' Him, ' because it seeth Him not, neither knoweth Him '; because they resist Him, and will not permit Him to work in their hearts. And then Jesus added, ' but ye know Him; for He dwelleth with you.' He had begun His work in them, but there was more to follow, for Jesus said, ' and shall be in you ' (John xiv. 17).

When a man is building himself a house, he is in and out of it and round about it. But we do not say he lives in it until it has been completed. And it is in that sense that Jesus said, ' He dwelleth with you.' But when the house is finished, the owner sweeps out all the chips and saw-dust, scrubs the floor, lays down his carpets, hangs up his pictures, arranges his furniture, and moves in with his family. Then he is in the fullest sense within it. He abides there. Now, it is in that sense that Jesus meant that the Holy Spirit should be in them. This is fitly expressed in one of our songs:

> Holy Spirit, come, O come,
> Let Thy work in me be done!
> All that hinders shall be thrown aside;
> Make me fit to be Thy dwelling.

Previous to Pentecost He was with them, using the searching preaching of John the Baptist, and the life, the words, the example, the sufferings, and the death and resurrection of Jesus as instruments with which to fashion their hearts for His indwelling. As the truth was declared to them in the words of Jesus, pictured to them in His doings, exemplified in His daily life, and fulfilled in His death and His rising from the dead, the Holy Spirit wrought mightily within them; but He could not yet find perfect rest in their hearts; therefore He did not yet abide within them.

They had forsaken all to follow Christ. They had been commissioned to preach the gospel, to heal the sick, to cleanse the lepers, to raise the dead, to cast out devils. Their names were written in Heaven. They were not of the world, even as Jesus was not of the world, for they belonged to Him and to the Father. They knew the Holy Spirit, for He was with them, working in them, but not yet living in them, for they were yet carnal; that is, they were selfish, each seeking the best place for himself. They disputed among themselves as to which should be the greatest. They were bigoted, wanting to call down fire from Heaven to consume those who would not receive Jesus, and forbidding those who would not follow them to cast out devils in His name. They were positive and loud in their professions of devotion and loyalty to Jesus when alone with Him. They declared they would die with Him. But they were fearful, timid and false to Him when the testing time came. When the mocking crowd appeared and danger was near, they all forsook Him and fled; while Peter cursed and swore, and denied that he knew Him.

But the Holy Spirit did not forsake them. He still wrought within them and, no doubt, used their very mistakes and miserable failures to perfect within them the spirit of humility and perfect self-abasement in order that they might safely be exalted. And on the day of Pentecost His work of preparation was complete, and He moved in to abide for ever. Hallelujah!

And this experience of theirs before Pentecost is the common experience of all true converts. Every child of God knows that the Holy Spirit is with him; realizes that He is working within, striving to set the house in order. And with many who are properly taught and gladly obedient this work is done quickly, and the heavenly Dove, the Blessed One, takes up His constant abode within them; the toil and strife with inbred sin is ended by its destruction, and they enter at once into the sabbath of full salvation.

Surely this is possible. The disciples could not receive the Holy Spirit till Jesus was glorified; because not until then was the foundation for perfect, intelligent, unwavering faith laid. But since the day of Pentecost, He may be received immediately by those who have repented of all sin, who have believed on Jesus and been born again. Some have assured me that they were sanctified wholly and filled with the Spirit within a few hours of their conversion. I have no doubt that this was so with many of the three thousand who were converted under Peter's preaching on the day of Pentecost.

But often this work is slow, for He can only work effectually as we work with Him, practising intelligent and obedient faith. Some days the work prospers and seems almost complete, and then peace and joy and comfort abound in the heart; at other times the work is hindered, and oftentimes almost or quite undone, by the strivings and stirrings of inbred sin, by fits of temper, by lightness and frivolity, by neglect of watchfulness

and prayer, and the patient, attentive study of His word;
by worldliness, by unholy ambitions, by jealousies and
envyings, by uncharitable suspicions and harsh judgments and selfish indulgences, and slowness to believe.

'The flesh lusteth against the Spirit' (Gal. v. 17),
seeks to bring the soul back under the bondage of sin
again, while the Spirit wars against the flesh, which is
'the old man', 'the carnal mind'. The Spirit seeks to
bring every thought into 'captivity . . . to the obedience
of Christ', to lead the soul to that point of glad, whole-
hearted consecration to its Lord, and that simple, perfect faith in the merits of His Blood which shall enable
Him to cast out 'the old man', destroy 'the carnal
mind' and, making the heart His temple, enthrone
Christ within.

> Here on earth a temple stands,
> Temple never built with hands;
> There the Lord doth fill the place
> With the glory of His grace.
> Cleansed by Christ's atoning Blood,
> *Thou* art this fair house of God.
> Thoughts, desires, that enter there,
> Should they not be pure and fair?
> Meet for holy courts and blest,
> Courts of stillness and of rest,
> Where the soul, a priest in white,
> Singeth praises day and night;
> Glory of the love divine,
> Filling all this heart of mine.

My brother, my sister, what is your experience just
now? Are you filled with the Spirit? Or is the old
man still warring against Him in your heart? Oh,
that you may receive Him fully by faith just now!

'HAVE YE RECEIVED THE HOLY GHOST SINCE YE
BELIEVED?'

CHAPTER III

Is the Baptism with the Holy Spirit a Third Blessing?

'Ye shall receive power, after that the Holy Ghost is come upon you.'

THERE is much difference of opinion among many of God's children as to the time and order of the baptism with the Holy Spirit, and many who believe that entire cleansing is subsequent to salvation ask if the baptism with the Spirit is not subsequent to cleansing and, therefore, a third blessing.

There are four classes of teachers whose views appear to differ about this subject. There are:

1. Those who emphasize cleansing; who say much of a clean heart, but little, if anything, about the fullness of the Holy Spirit and power from on high.

2. Those who emphasize the baptism with the Holy Ghost and fullness of the Spirit, but say little or nothing of cleansing from inbred sin and the destruction of the carnal mind.

3. Those who say much of both, but separate them into two distinct experiences, often widely separated in time.

4. Those who teach that the truth is in the union of the two, and that, while we may separate them in their order, putting cleansing first, we cannot separate them as to time, since it is the baptism that cleanses, just as the darkness vanishes before the flash of the electric light when the right button is touched; just as the Augean stables were cleansed, in the fabled story of Grecian mythology, when Hercules turned in the floods of the River Arno; the refuse went out as the rushing waters poured in.

In John xvii. 15-26 Jesus prays for His disciples, and says: ' I pray not that Thou shouldest take them out of the world, but that Thou shouldest keep them from the evil. . . . Sanctify them . . . that they all may be one; as Thou, Father, art in Me, and I in Thee, that they also may be one in Us . . . I in them, and Thou in Me, that they may be made perfect in one . . . that the love wherewith Thou hast loved Me may be in them, and I in them.'

It is first sanctification (cleansing, being made holy), then filling, divine union with the Father and the Son through the Holy Spirit.

The Scriptures make plain the order of God's work, and if we looked at them alone, without diligently comparing Scripture with Scripture, as God would have us do, we might perhaps conclude that the cleansing and filling were as distinct and separate in time as they are in this order of statement.

But other Scriptures give us abundant light on that side of the subject. In Acts x. 44 we read of Peter's preaching Jesus to Cornelius, the Roman centurion, and his household; and ' while Peter yet spake these words, the Holy Ghost fell on all them which heard the word '; and in Acts xv. 7-9, at the Council in Jerusalem, we have Peter's rehearsal of the experience of Cornelius and his household. Peter says: ' Men and brethren, ye know how that a good while ago God made choice among us, that the Gentiles by my mouth should hear the word of the gospel, and believe. And God, which knoweth the hearts, bare them witness, giving them the Holy Ghost, even as He did unto us; And put no difference between us and them, purifying their hearts by faith.' Here we see that their believing, and the sudden descent of the Holy Ghost with cleansing power into their hearts, constitute one blessed experience.

What patient, waiting, expectant faith reckons done, the baptism with the Holy Ghost actually accomplishes. Between the act of faith by which a man begins to reckon himself 'dead indeed unto sin, but alive unto God through Jesus Christ our Lord ' (Rom. vi. 11), and the act of the Holy Spirit, which makes the reckoning good, there may be an interval of time; but the act and state of steadfastly, patiently, joyously, perfectly believing, which is man's part, and the act of baptizing with the Holy Ghost, cleansing as by fire, which is God's part, bring about the one experience of entire sanctification, and must not and cannot be logically looked upon as two distinct blessings, any more than the act of the husband and the act of the wife can be separated in the one experience of marriage.

There are two works and two workers: God and man. Just as my right arm and my left arm work when my two hands come together, but the union of the two hands constitute one experience.

If my left arm acts quickly, my right arm will surely respond. And so, if the soul, renouncing self and sin and the world, with ardour of faith in the precious Blood for cleansing and in the promise of the gift of the Holy Spirit, draws nigh to God, God will draw nigh to that soul, and the blessed union will be effected suddenly. In that instant, what faith has reckoned done will be done, the death-stroke will be given to ' the old man ', sin will die, and the heart will be clean and wholly alive toward God through our Lord Jesus Christ. It will not be a mere ' make-believe ' experience, but a gloriously real one.

It is possible that some have been led into confusion of thought on this subject by not considering all the Scriptures bearing on it. What is it that cleanses or sanctifies, and how? Jesus prays: ' Sanctify them through Thy truth: Thy word is truth ' (John xvii. 17). Here it is the word, or truth, that sanctifies.

John says: ' The blood of Jesus Christ His Son cleanseth us from all sin ' (1 John i. 7). Here it is the Blood.

Peter says: ' God . . . put no difference between us

and them, purifying their hearts by faith ' (Acts xv. 8, 9).
And Paul says: ' That they may receive forgiveness of
sins, and inheritance among them which are sanctified
by faith ' (Acts xxvi. 18).   Here it is by faith.

Again, Paul writes: ' God hath from the beginning
chosen you to salvation through sanctification of the
Spirit ' (2 Thess. ii. 13).   And again, ' That the offering
up of the Gentiles might be acceptable, being sanctified
by the Holy Ghost ' (Rom. xv. 16).   And Peter writes:
' To the strangers . . . elect . . . through sanctification
of the Spirit ' (1 Pet. i. 1, 2).   Here it is the Spirit that
sanctifies or makes clean and holy.

Is there, then, confusion here? Jesus says, ' the truth ';
John says, ' the Blood '; Paul and Peter say, ' faith ',
and ' the Holy Ghost '.   Can these be reconciled?   Let
us see.

Here is a child in a burning house.   A man at the
peril of his life rushes to the spot above which the child
stands in awful danger, and cries out, ' Jump, and I
will catch you! '

The child hears, believes, leaps, and the man receives
him; but just as he turns and places the boy in safety, a
falling timber smites him to the ground wounded to
death, and his flowing blood sprinkles the boy whom he
has saved.

A breathless spectator says: ' The child's faith saved
him.'   Another says: ' How quick the lad was!   His
courageous leap saved him.'   Another says: ' Bless the
child!   He was in awful danger, and he just barely saved
himself.'   Another says: ' That man's word just reached
the boy's ear in the nick of time, and saved him.'
Another says: ' God bless that man!   He saved that
child.'   And yet another says: ' That boy was saved by
blood; by the sacrifice of that heroic man! '

Now, what saved the child?   Without the man's
presence and promise there would have been no faith;
and without faith there would have been no saving
action and the boy would have perished.   The man's

word saved him by inspiring faith. Faith saved him by leading to proper action. He saved himself by leaping. The man saved him by sacrificing his own life in order to catch him when he leaped.

Not the child himself alone, nor his faith, nor his brave leap, nor his rescuer's word, nor his blood, nor the man himself saved the boy, but they all together saved him; and the boy was not saved till he was in the arms of the man.

And so it is faith and works, and the word and the Blood and the Holy Ghost that sanctify.

The Blood, the sacrifice of Christ, underlies all, and is the meritorious cause of every blessing we receive, but the Holy Spirit is the active agent by whom the merits of the Blood are applied to our needs.

During the American Civil War certain men committed some dastardly and unlawful deeds, and were sentenced to be shot. On the day of the execution they stood in a row confronted by soldiers with loaded muskets, waiting the command to fire. Just before the command was given, the commanding officer felt a touch on his elbow and, turning, saw a young man by his side, who said, ' Sir, there in that row, waiting to be shot, is a married man. He has a wife and children. He is their bread-winner. If you shoot him, he will be sorely missed. *Let me take his place.*'

' All right,' said the officer; ' take his place, if you wish; but you will be shot.'

' I quite understand that,' replied the young man; ' but no one will miss me.' And, going to the condemned man, he pushed him aside, and took his place.

Soon the command to fire was given. The volley rang out, and the young hero dropped dead with a bullet through his heart, while the other man went free.

His freedom came to him by blood. Had he, however, neglected the great salvation and, despising the blood shed for him and refusing the sacrifice of the friend and the righteous claims of the law, persisted in the same evil ways, he, too, would have been shot. The blood, though shed for him, would not have availed to set him free. But he accepted the sacrifice, submitted to the law, and went home to his wife and children. It was by the blood; every breath he henceforth drew, every throb of his heart, every blessing he enjoyed, or possibly could enjoy, came to him by the blood. He owed everything from that day forth to the blood, and every fleeting moment, every passing day and every rolling year but increased his debt to the blood which had been shed for him.

And so we owe all to the Blood of Christ, for we were under sentence of death—' The soul that sinneth, it shall die' (Ezek. xviii. 20)—and we have all sinned, and God, to be holy, must frown upon sin and utterly condemn it, and must execute His sentence against it.

But Jesus suffered for our sins. He died for us. ' He was wounded for our transgressions, He was bruised for our iniquities . . . and with His stripes we are healed ' (Isa. liii. 5). ' Ye know that ye were not redeemed with corruptible things, as silver and gold . . . but with the precious blood of Christ ' (1 Pet. i. 18, 19); ' Who loved me, and gave Himself for me ' (Gal. ii. 20). And now every blessing we ever had, or ever shall have, comes to us by the divine sacrifice, by ' the precious blood ', And ' How shall we escape, if we neglect so great salvation?' (Heb. ii. 3). His Blood is the meritorious cause not only of our pardon, but of our cleansing, our sanctification; but the Holy Spirit is the ever-present, living, active cause.

The truth or word which sanctifies is the record God has given us of His will and of that divine sacrifice, that ' precious blood '. The faith that purifies is that sure confidence in that word which leads to renunciation of all self-righteousness, that utter abandonment to God's will, and full dependence on the merits of ' the precious blood ', the ' faith that works by love ', for ' faith without works is dead '. And thus we draw nigh to God, and God draws nigh to us, and the Holy Ghost falls upon us, comes into us, and cleanses our hearts by the destruction of sin and the shedding abroad within us of the love of God.

The advocates of entire sanctification as an experience wrought in the soul by the baptism with the Spirit subsequent to regeneration call it ' the second blessing '.

But many good people object to the term, and say that they have received the first, second, third and fiftieth blessing, and no doubt they have, and yet the people who speak of ' the second blessing ' are right, in the sense in which they use the term; and in that sense there are but the two blessings.

Some years ago a man heard things about a lady that filled him with admiration for her, and made him feel that they were of one mind and heart. Later, he met her for the first time, and fell in love with her. After some months, following an enlarged acquaintance and much consideration and prayer, he told her of his love and asked her to become his wife; and after due consideration and prayer on her part she consented, and they promised themselves to each other; they plighted their faith, and in a sense gave themselves to each other.

That was the first blessing, and it filled him with great peace and joy, but not perfect peace and joy. Now, there were many blessings following that before the great second blessing came. Every letter he received, every tender look, every pressure of the hand, every tone of her voice, every fresh assurance of enduring and increasing affection was a blessing; but it was not the second blessing.

But one day, after patient waiting, which might have been shortened by mutual consent, if they had thought it wise, and after full preparation, they came together in the presence of friends and before a man of God, and in the most solemn and irrevocable manner gave themselves to each other to become one, and were pronounced man and wife. That was the second blessing, an epochal experience, unlike anything which preceded or anything to follow. And now their peace and joy and rest were full.

There had to be the first and second blessings in this relationship of man and wife, but there is no third. And yet in the sense of those who say they have received fifty blessings from the Lord, there have been countless blessings in the wedded life; indeed, it has been a river of blessing, broadening and deepening in gladness and joy and sweet affections and fellowship with the increasing years.

But let us not confuse thought by disputing over terms and wrangling about words.

The first blessing in Jesus Christ is salvation, with its negative side of remission of sins and forgiveness, and its positive side of renewal or regeneration—the new birth—one experience.

And the second blessing is entire sanctification, with its negative side of cleansing, and its positive side of filling with the Holy Ghost—one whole, rounded, glorious, epochal experience. And while there may be many refreshings, girdings, illuminations and secret tokens and assurances of love and favour, there is no third blessing in this large sense in this present time.

But when time is no more, when the everlasting doors have lifted up, and the King of Glory comes in with His Bride and, for ever redeemed and crowned, He makes us to sit down with Him on His throne, then in eternity we shall have the third blessing—we shall be glorified.

'HAVE YE RECEIVED THE HOLY GHOST SINCE YE BELIEVED?'

CHAPTER IV

The Witness of the Spirit

' Ye shall receive power, after that the Holy Ghost is come upon you.'

HOW shall I know that I am accepted of God?—
that I am saved or sanctified? The Bible declares
God's love and pity for sinners, including me, and
reveals His offer of mercy to me in Jesus Christ, on
condition that I fully repent of my sins and, yielding
myself to Him, believe on Jesus Christ and, taking up
my cross, follow Him. But how shall I know that I
have met these conditions in a way to satisfy Him, and
that I am myself saved?

1. The Bible cannot tell me this. It tells me what to
do, but it does not tell me when I have done it, any more
than the sign-board at the country cross-roads, pointing
out the road leading to the city, tells me when I have
reached the city.

2. My religious teachers and friends cannot tell me,
for they cannot read my heart, nor the mind of God
toward me. How can they know when I have in my
heart repented and believed, and when His righteous
anger is turned away? They can encourage me to
repent, believe, obey, and can assure me that, if I do, He
will accept me and I shall be saved; but beyond that
they cannot go.

3. My own heart, owing to its darkness and deceitfulness and liability to error, is not a safe witness previous
to the assurance God Himself gives. If my neighbour is
justly offended with me, it is not my own heart, but his
testimony that first assures me of his favour once more.

How, then, shall I know that I am justified or wholly

sanctified? There is but one way, and that is by the witness of the Holy Spirit. God must notify me, and make me to know it; and this He does when, despairing of my own works of righteousness, I cast my poor soul fully and in faith upon Jesus. Says Paul: ' Ye have not received the spirit of bondage again to fear; but ye have received the Spirit of adoption, whereby we cry, Abba, Fathei. The Spirit itself beareth witness with our spirit, that we are the children of God ' (Rom. viii. 15, 16). ' And because ye are sons, God hath sent forth the Spirit of His Son into your hearts, crying, Abba, Father ' (Gal. iv. 6). Unless He Himself assures me, I shall never know that He accepts me, but must continue in uncertainty all my days.

> Come, Holy Ghost, Thyself impress
> On my expanding heart;
> And show that in the Father's grace
> I share a filial part.

The Founder says: ' Assurance is produced by the revelation of forgiveness and acceptance made by God Himself directly to the soul. This is the witness of the Spirit. It is God testifying in my soul that He has loved me and given Himself for me, and washed me from my sins in His own Blood. Nothing short of this *actual revelation*, made by God Himself, can make anyone sure of salvation.'

John Wesley says: ' By the testimony of the Spirit, I mean an inward impression of the soul, whereby the Spirit of God immediately and directly witnesses to mv spirit that I am a child of God; that Jesus hath loved me, and given Himself for me; that all my sins are blotted out, and I, even I, am reconciled to God.'

This witness of the Spirit addressed to my consciousness enables me to sing with joyful assurance:

> My God is reconciled,
> His pardoning voice I hear;
> He owns me for His child,
> I can no longer fear;
> With confidence I now draw nigh
> And Father, Abba Father! cry.

When the Holy Spirit witnesses to me that I am saved and adopted into God's family as His child, then other evidences begin to abound also. For instance:

1. My own spirit witnesses that I am a new creature. I know that old things have passed away and all things have become new. My very thoughts and desires have been changed. Love and joy and peace reign within me. My heart no longer condemns me. Pride and selfishness, and lust and temper, no longer control my thoughts nor lead captive my will. I am a new creature, and I know it, and I infer without doubt that this is the work of God in me.

2. My conscience bears witness that I am honest and true in all my purposes and intentions; that I am without guile; that my eye is single to the glory of God, and that with all simplicity and sincerity of heart I serve Him; and, since by nature I am only sinful, I again infer that this sincerity of heart is His blessed work in my soul and is a fruit of salvation.

3. The Bible becomes a witness to my salvation. In it are accurately portrayed the true characteristics of the children of God; and as I study it prayerfully, and find these characteristics in my heart and life, I again infer that I am saved. This is true self-examination and is most useful.

These evidences are most important to guard us against any mistake as to the witness of the Holy Spirit.

The witness of the Spirit is not likely to be mistaken for something else, just as the sun is not likely to be mistaken for a lesser light, a glow-worm or a moon. But one who has not seen the sun might mistake some lesser light for the sun. So an unsaved man may mistake some flash of fancy, some pleasant emotion, for the witness of the Spirit. But if he is honest, the absence of these secondary evidences and witnesses will correct him. He must know that so long as sin masters him, reigns within him, and he is devoid of the tempers, graces and dispositions of God's people as portrayed in the Bible, that he is mistaken in supposing that he has the witness of the Spirit. The Holy Spirit cannot witness to what does not exist. He cannot lie. Not until sin is forgiven does He witness to the fact. Not until we are justified from our old sins and born again does He witness that we are children of God; and when He does so witness, these secondary evidences always follow. Charles Wesley expresses this in one of his matchless hymns:

> How can a sinner know
>   His sins on earth forgiven?
> How can my gracious Saviour show
>   My name inscribed in Heaven?
>
> We who in Christ believe
>   That He for us hath died,
> We all His unknown peace receive,
>   And feel His Blood applied.
>
> His love, surpassing far
>   The love of all beneath,
> We find within our hearts, and dare
>   The pointless darts of death.
>
> Stronger than death and Hell
>   The mystic power we prove;
> And, conquerors of the world, we dwell
>   In Heaven, who dwell in love.

The witness of the Spirit is far more comprehensive than many suppose. Multitudes do not believe that there is any such thing, while others confine it to the forgiveness of sins and adoption into the family of God. But the truth is that the Holy Spirit witnesses to much more than this.

He witnesses to the sinner that he is guilty, condemned before God, and lost. This we call conviction; but it is none other than the witness of the Spirit to the sinner's true condition; and when a man realizes it, nothing can convince him to the contrary. His friends may point out his good works, his kindly disposition, and try to assure him that he is not a bad man; but, so long as the Spirit continues to witness to his guilt, nothing can console him or reassure his quaking heart. This con-victing witness may come to a sinner at any time, but it is usually given under the searching preaching of the gospel, or the burning testimony of those who have been gloriously saved and sanctified; or in time of danger, when the soul is awed into silence so that it can hear the ' still small voice ' of the Holy Spirit.

Again, the Holy Spirit not only witnesses to the for-giveness of sins and acceptance with God, but He also witnesses to sanctification. ' For by one offering He (that is, Jesus) hath perfected for ever them that are sanctified. Whereof the Holy Ghost also is a witness to us ' (Heb. x. 14, 15).

Indeed, one who has this witness can no more doubt it than a man with two good eyes can doubt the existence of the sun when he steps forth into the splendour of a cloudless noonday. It satisfies him, and he cries out exultingly, ' We know, we know! ' Hallelujah!

Paul seems to teach that the Holy Spirit witnesses to every good thing God works in us, for he says: ' We have received, not the spirit of the world, but the Spirit which is of God; that we might know the things that are freely given to us of God ' (1 Cor. ii. 12). It is for our comfort and encouragement to know our acceptance of God and our rights, privileges and possessions in Jesus Christ; and the Holy Spirit is given for this purpose, that we may *know*.

But it is important to bear in mind God's plan of work in this matter.

1. The witness of the Spirit is dependent upon our faith. God does not give it to those who do not believe in Jesus; and if our faith wavers, the witness will become intermittent; and if faith fails, it will be withdrawn. Owing to the unsteadiness of their faith, many young converts get into uncertainty. Happy are they at such times if someone is at hand to instruct and encourage them to look steadfastly to Jesus. But, alas! many old Christians through unsteady faith walk in gloom and

uncertainty and, instead of encouraging the young, they discourage them. Steadfast faith will keep the inward witness bright.

2. We must not take our attention off Jesus, and the promises of God in Him, and fix it upon the witness of the Spirit. The witness continues only while we look unto Jesus and trust and obey Him. When we take our eyes off Him, the witness is gone. Many people fail here. Instead of quietly and confidently looking unto Jesus and trusting Him, they are vainly looking for the witness; which is as though a man should try to realize the sweetness of honey, without receiving it in his mouth; or the beauty of a picture, while having his eyes turned inward upon himself instead of outward upon the picture. Jesus saves. Look to Him, and He will send the Spirit to witness to His work.

3. The witness may be brightened by diligence in the discharge of duty, by frequent seasons of glad prayer, by definite testimony to salvation and sanctification, and by stirring up our faith.

4. The witness may be dulled by neglect of duty, by sloth in prayer, by inattention to the Bible, by indefinite, hesitating testimony, and by carelessness, when we should be careful to walk soberly and steadfastly with the Lord.

5. I dare not say that the witness of the Spirit is dependent upon our health, but there are some forms of nervous and organic disease that seem so to distract or becloud the mind as to interfere with the clear discernment of the witness of the Spirit. I knew a nervous little child who would be so distracted with fear by an approaching carriage, when being carried across the street in her father's arms, that she seemed to be incapable of hearing or heeding his reassuring voice. It may be that there are some diseases that for the time prevent the sufferer from discerning the reassuring witness of the heavenly Father. Dr. Asa Mahan told me of an experience of this kind which he had in a very dangerous sickness. And Dr. Daniel Steele had a similar

experience while lying at the point of death with typhoid fever. But some of the happiest Christians the world has seen have been racked with pain and tortured with disease.

And so there may be seasons of fierce temptation when the witness is not clearly discerned; but we may rest assured that if our hearts cleave to Jesus Christ and duty, He will never leave or forsake us. Blessed be God!

6. But the witness will be lost if we wilfully sin, or persistently neglect to follow where He leads. This witness is a pearl of great price, and Satan will try to steal it from us; therefore, we must guard it with watchful prayer continually.

7. If lost, it may be found again by prayer and faith and a dutiful taking up of the cross which has been laid down. Thousands who have lost it have found it again, and often they have found it with increased brightness and glory. If you have lost it, my brother, look up in faith to your loving God, and He will restore it to you. It is possible to live on the right side of plain duty without the witness, but you cannot be sure of your salvation, joyful in service, or glad in God, without it; and since it is promised to all God's children, no one who professes to be His should be without it.

If you have it not, my brother or sister, seek it now by faith in Jesus. Go to Him, and do not let Him go till He notifies you that you are His. Listen to Charles Wesley:

> From the world of sin and noise
>   And hurry, I withdraw;
> For the small and inward voice
>   I wait with humble awe;
> Silent am I now and still,
>   Dare not in Thy presence move;
> To my waiting soul reveal
>   The secret of Thy love.

Do you want the witness to abide? Then study the word of God and live by it; sing and make melody in your heart to the Lord; praise the Lord with your first waking breath in the morning, and thank Him with your last waking breath at night; flee from sin; keep on believing; look to Jesus, cleave to Him, follow Him gladly, trust the efficacy of His Blood, and the witness will abide in your heart. Be patient with the Lord. Let Him mould you, and 'He will save, He will rejoice over thee with joy; He will rest in His love, He will joy over thee with singing' (Zeph. iii. 17); and you shall no longer doubt, but know that you are His. Hallelujah!

> There are in this loud stunning tide
>   Of human care and crime,
> With whom the melodies abide
>   Of th' everlasting chime,
> Who carry music in their heart
>   Through dusky lane and wrangling mart,
> Plying their task with busier feet
> Because their secret souls a holy strain repeat.

And that 'holy strain' is but the echo of the Lord's song in their heart, which is the witness of the Spirit.

'HAVE YE RECEIVED THE HOLY GHOST SINCE YE BELIEVED?'

CHAPTER V

Purity

' Ye shall receive power, after that the Holy Ghost is come upon you.

A MINISTER of the gospel, after listening to an eminent servant of God preaching on entire sanctification through the baptism with the Spirit, wrote to him, saying: ' I like your teaching on the baptism with the Holy Ghost. I need it and am seeking it; but I do not care much for entire sanctification or heart-cleansing. Pray for me that I may be filled with the Holy Ghost.'

The brother knew him well, and immediately replied: ' I am so glad you believe in the baptism with the Holy Ghost, and are so earnestly seeking it. I join my prayer with yours that you may receive that gift. But let me say to you, that if you get the gift of the Holy Ghost, you will have to take entire sanctification with it, for the first thing the baptism with the Holy Ghost does is to cleanse the heart from all sin.'

Thank God, he humbled himself, permitted the Lord to sanctify him, and he was filled with the Holy Spirit and mightily empowered to work for God.

Many have looked at the promise of power when the Holy Ghost is come, the energy of Peter's preaching on the day of Pentecost, and the marvellous results which followed; and they have hastily and erroneously jumped to the conclusion that the baptism with the Holy Ghost is for work and service only.

It does bring power—the power of God—and it does fit for service, probably the most important service to which any created beings are commissioned, the proclamation of salvation and the conditions of peace to a

31

lost world; but not that alone, nor primarily. The primary, the basal work of the baptism, is that of cleansing.

You may turn a flood into your millrace, but until it sweeps away the logs and brushwood and dirt that obstruct the course, you cannot get power to turn the wheels of your mill. The flood first washes out the obstructions, and then you have power.

The great hindrance in the hearts of God's children to the power of the Holy Ghost is inbred sin—that dark, defiant, evil something within that struggles for the mastery of the soul, and will not submit to be meek and lowly, patient, forbearing and holy, as was Jesus; and when the Holy Spirit comes, His first work is to sweep away that something, that carnal principle, and make free and clean all the channels of the soul.

Peter was filled with power on the day of Pentecost; but evidently the purifying effect of the baptism made a deeper and more lasting impression upon his mind than the empowering effect; for years after, in the Council in Jerusalem, recorded in the fifteenth chapter of Acts, he stood up and told about the spiritual baptism of Cornelius, the Roman centurion, and his household, and said: ' And God, which knoweth the hearts, bare them witness, giving them the Holy Ghost, even as He did unto us; And put no difference between us and them, purifying their hearts by faith ' (verses 8, 9). Here he calls attention not to power, but to purity, as the effect of the baptism. When the Holy Ghost comes in to abide ' the old man ' goes out. Praise the Lord!

This destruction of inbred sin is made perfectly plain in that wonderful Old Testament type of the baptism with the Holy Ghost and fire recorded in the sixth chapter of Isaiah. The prophet was a most earnest preacher of righteousness (see Isa. i. 10-20), yet he was not sanctified wholly. But he had a vision of the Lord upon His throne, and the seraphims crying one to another: ' Holy, holy, holy, is the Lord of hosts: the whole earth is full of

His glory.' And the very ' posts of the door moved at
the voice of him that cried '; and how much more should
the heart of the prophet be moved! And so it was; and
he cried out: ' Woe is me! for I am undone; because
I am a man of unclean lips, and I dwell in the midst of a
people of unclean lips: for mine eyes have seen the King,
the Lord of hosts.'

When unsanctified men have a vision of God, it is
not their lack of power, but their lack of purity, their
unlikeness to Christ, the Holy One, that troubles them.
And so it was with the prophet. But he adds: ' Then
flew one of the seraphims unto me, having a live coal in
his hand, which he had taken with the tongs from off
the altar: And he laid it upon my mouth, and said, Lo,
this hath touched thy lips; and thine iniquity is taken
away, and thy sin purged ' (verses 6, 7). Here again,
it is purity rather than power to which our attention
is directed.

Again, in the thirty-sixth chapter of Ezekiel, we have
another type of this spiritual baptism. In Isaiah the
type was that of fire, but here it is that of water; for
water and oil, and the wind and rain and dew, are all
used as types of the Holy Spirit.

The Lord says, through Ezekiel: 'Then will I sprinkle
clean water upon you, and ye shall be clean: from all
your filthiness, and from all your idols, will I cleanse
you. A new heart also will I give you, and a new spirit
will I put within you: and I will take away the stony
heart out of your flesh, and I will give you an heart of
flesh. And I will put My Spirit within you, and cause
you to walk in My statutes, and ye shall keep My judgments, and do them.'

Here again, the incoming of the Holy Spirit means the
outgoing of all sin, of ' all your filthiness, and from all
your idols '. How plainly it is taught! And yet, many
of God's dear children do not believe it is their privilege
to be free from sin and pure in heart in this life. But, may
we not? Let us consider this.

1. It is certainly *desirable*. Every sincere Christian—and none can be a Christian who is not sincere—wants to be free from sin, to be pure in heart, to be like Christ. Sin is hateful to every true child of God. The Spirit within him cries out against the sin, the wrong temper, the pride, the lust, the selfishness, the evil that lurks within the heart. Surely, it is desirable to be free from sin.

> He wills that I should holy be;
>   That holiness I long to feel,
> That full divine conformity
>   To all my Saviour's righteous will.

2. It is *necessary*, for without holiness ' no man shall see the Lord'. Sometime, somehow, somewhere, sin must go out of our hearts—all sin—or we cannot go into Heaven. Sin would spoil Heaven just as it spoils earth; just as it spoils the peace of hearts and homes, of families and neighbourhoods and nations here. Why God in His wisdom allows sin in the world, I do not know, I cannot understand. But this I understand: that He has one world into which He will not let sin enter. He has notified us in advance that no sin, nothing that defiles, can enter Heaven, can mar the blessedness of that holy place. ' Who shall ascend into the hill of the Lord? or who shall stand in His holy place? He that hath clean hands, and a pure heart; who hath not lifted up his soul unto vanity, nor sworn deceitfully' (Ps. xxiv. 3, 4). We must get rid of sin to get into Heaven, to enjoy the full favour of God. It is necessary.

> Choose I must, and soon must choose
> Holiness, or Heaven lose.
> If what Heaven loves I hate,
> Shut for me is Heaven's gate.

> Endless sin means endless woe;
> Into endless sin I go
> If my soul, from reason rent,
> Takes from sin its final bent.

As the stream its channel grooves,
And within that channel·moves;
So does habit's deepest tide
Groove its bed and there abide.

Light obeyed increaseth light;
Light resisted bringeth night;
Who shall give me will to choose
If the love of light I lose?

Speed, my soul, this instant yield;
Let the light its sceptre wield.
While thy God prolongs His grace,
Haste thee to His holy face.

3. This purification from sin is *promised*. Nothing can
be plainer than the promise of God on this point.
' Then will I sprinkle clean water upon you, and ye shall
be clean: from all your filthiness, and from all your
idols, will I cleanse you.' When all is removed, nothing
remains. When all filthiness and all idols are taken
away, none are left.

' But where sin abounded, grace did much more
abound: That as sin hath reigned unto death, even so
might grace reign through righteousness unto eternal
life by Jesus Christ our Lord ' (Rom. v. 20, 21). Grace
reigns, not through sin, but ' through righteousness '
which has expelled sin. Grace brings in righteousness
and sin goes out.

' If we walk in the light, as He is in the light, we have
fellowship one with another, and the blood of Jesus
Christ His Son cleanseth us from all sin ' (1 John i. 7).
Hallelujah!

' Being then made free from sin, ye became the servants of righteousness ' (Rom. vi. 18).

These are sample promises and assurances any one of
which is sufficient to encourage us to believe that our
heavenly Father will save us from all sin, if we meet
His conditions.

4. Deliverance is *possible*. It was for this that Jesus
Christ, the Father's Son, came into the world, and suffered

and died, that He might 'save His people from their sins' (Matt. i. 21). It was for this that He shed His precious Blood to 'cleanse us from all sin'. It was for this that the word of God, with its wonderful promises, was given, 'that by these ye might be partakers of the divine nature, having escaped the corruption that is in the world through lust' (2 Pet. i. 4); by which is meant escape from inbred sin. It was for this that ministers of the gospel—Salvation Army officers—are given, 'for the perfecting of the saints' (Eph. iv. 12), for the saving and sanctifying of men (Acts xxvi. 18). It is primarily for this that the Holy Ghost comes as a baptism of fire: that sin might be consumed out of us, so that we might be made meet for 'the inheritance of the saints in light' (Col. 1. 12); that so we might be ready without a moment's warning to go into the midst of the heavenly hosts in white garments, 'washed in the Blood of the Lamb'. Glory be to God for ever and ever!

And shall all these mighty agents and this heavenly provision, and these gracious purposes of God, fail to destroy sin out of any obedient, believing heart? Is sin omnipotent? No!

If you, my brother, my sister, will look unto Jesus just now, trusting the merits of His Blood, and receive the Holy Spirit into your heart, you shall be 'made free from sin'; it 'shall not have dominion over you'. Hallelujah! Under the fiery touch of His holy presence, your iniquity shall be taken away, and your sin shall be purged. And you yourself shall burn as did the bush on the mount of God which Moses saw; yet you, like the bush, shall not be consumed; and by this holy fire, this flame of love, that consumes sin, you shall be made proof against that unquenchable fire that consumes sinners.

> Come, Holy Ghost, Thy mighty aid bestowing!
> Destroy the works of sin, the self, the pride;
> Burn, burn in me, my idols overthrowing;
> Prepare my heart for Him, for my Lord crucified.

'HAVE YE RECEIVED THE HOLY GHOST SINCE YE BELIEVED?'

CHAPTER VI

Power

Ye shall receive power, after that the Holy Ghost is come upon you.'

JUST before His ascension, Jesus met His disciples for the last time, and repeated His command that they should ' not depart from Jerusalem, but wait for the promise of the Father ', and reiterated His promise that they should be ' baptized with the Holy Ghost not many days hence '.

Then ' they asked of Him, saying, Lord, wilt Thou at this time restore again the kingdom to Israel? ' They were still eager for an earthly kingdom. But ' He said unto them, It is not for you to know the times or the seasons, which the Father hath put in His own power ', or authority. And then He added, ' But ye shall receive power, after that the Holy Ghost is come upon you ' (Acts 1. 4-8).

They wanted power, and He assured them that they should have it, but said nothing of its nature, or the work and activities into which it would thrust them, and for which it would equip them, beyond the fact that they should be witnesses unto Him ' in Jerusalem, and in all Judaea, and in Samaria, and unto the uttermost part of the earth '. After that the Holy Ghost Himself was henceforth to be their Teacher.

And then Jesus left them. Earth lost its power to hold Him, and while they beheld Him He began to ascend; a cloud bent low from Heaven, receiving Him out of sight, and they were left alone, with His promise of power ringing in their ears, and His command to ' wait for the promise of the Father ' checking any impatience

37

that might lead them to ' go a-fishing ', as Peter had done some days before, or cause an undue haste to begin their life-work of witnessing for Him before God's appointed time.

For ten days they waited, not listlessly, but eagerly, as a maid for her mistress, or a servant for his master, who is expected to come at any moment; they forgot their personal ambitions; they ceased to judge and criticize one another, and in the sweet unity of brotherly love, ' with one accord ' they rejoiced, they prayed, they waited; and then on the day of Pentecost, at their early morning prayer meeting, when they were all present, the windows of Heaven were opened, and such a blessing as they could not contain was poured out upon them. 'And suddenly there came a sound from Heaven as of a rushing mighty wind, and it filled all the house where they were sitting. And there appeared unto them cloven tongues like as of fire, and it sat upon each of them. And they were all filled with the Holy Ghost.'

This was the inaugural day of the Church of God (Acts ii. 2-4); the dawn of the dispensation of the Holy Spirit; the beginning of the days of power.

In the morning of that day there were only a few Christians in the world; the New Testament was not written, and it is doubtful if they had among them all a copy of the Old Testament; they had no church build-ings, no colleges, no religious books and papers; they were poor and despised, unlearned and ignorant; but before night they had enrolled three thousand converts, and they had aroused and filled all Jerusalem with questionings and amazement.

What was the secret? Power. What was the secret? God the Holy Ghost. He had come, and this work was His work, and they were His instruments.

When Jesus came, a body was prepared for Him (Heb. x. 5), and through that body He wrought His wondrous works; but when the other Comforter comes,

He takes possession of those bodies that are freely and fully presented to Him, and He touches their lips with grace; He shines peacefully and gloriously on their faces; He flashes beams of pity and compassion and heavenly affection from their eyes; He kindles a fire of love in their hearts, and lights the flame of truth in their minds. They become His temple, and their hearts are a holy of holies in which His blessed presence ever abides; and from that central citadel He works, enduing the man who has received Him with power.

If you ask how the Holy Spirit can dwell within us and work through us without destroying our personality, I cannot tell. How can electric impulses fill and transform a dead wire into a live one which you dare not touch? How can a magnetic current fill a piece of steel, and transform it into a mighty force which by its touch can raise tons of iron, as a child would lift a feather? How can fire dwell in a piece of iron until its very appearance is that of fire, and it becomes a firebrand? I cannot tell.

Now, what fire and electricity and magnetism do in iron and steel, the Holy Spirit does in the spirits of men who believe on Jesus, follow Him wholly and trust Him intelligently. He dwells in them and inspires them, till they are all alive with the very life of God.

The transformation wrought in men by the baptism with the Holy Ghost, and the power that fills them, are amazing beyond measure. The Holy Spirit gives:

1. *Power over the world.* They become

> Dead to the world and all its toys,
> Its idle pomp and fading joys.

The world masters and enslaves people who have not the Holy Spirit. To one man it offers money. He falls down and worships; he sells his conscience and character for gold. To another it offers power. He falls down and worships; he sacrifices his principles and sears his conscience for power. To another it offers pleasure; to another learning; to another fame; they fall down and worship, and sell themselves for these things. But the man filled with the Holy Ghost is free. He can turn from these things without a pang, as he would from pebbles; or, he can take them and use them as his servants for the glory of God and the good of men.

What did Peter and James and John care for the great places in the kingdoms of this world after they were filled with the Holy Ghost? They would not have exchanged places with Herod the king or with Caesar himself. For the gratification of any personal ambition these things were no more attractive to them now than the lordship over a tribe of ants on their tiny hill. They were now kings and priests unto God, and theirs was an everlasting Kingdom, and its glory exceeds the glory of the kingdoms of this world as the splendour of the sun exceeds that of the glow-worm.

The head of some great business enterprises was making many thousands of dollars every year; but when the Holy Spirit filled him money lost its power over him. He still retained his position, and made vast sums; but, as a steward of the Lord, he poured it into God's work, and has been doing so for more than thirty years.

After Pentecost the disciples in Jerusalem held all their possessions in common, so completely were they freed from the power and love of money.

A rising young lawyer got filled with the Spirit, and the next day said to his client: ' I cannot plead your case. I have a retainer from the Lord Jesus '; and he became one of the mightiest preachers the world has ever seen.

A popular lad got the fiery baptism, and went to his baseball team and said: ' Boys, you swear, and I am now a Christian; I cannot play with you any more.' God made him the wonder of all his old friends, and a happy winner of souls.

A fashionable woman got the baptism, and God gave her power to break away from her worldly set and

surroundings, live wholly for Him, and gave her an
influence that girdled the globe.

Paul said: ' The world is crucified unto me, and I unto
the world ' (Gal. vi. 14). Men could whip and stone and
imprison his body, and cut off his head, but his soul was
free. It was enslaved and driven by no unholy or
inordinate ambition, by no lust for gold, by no desire for
power or fame, by no fear of man, by no shame of worldly
censure or adverse public opinion. He had power over
the world; and this same power is the birthright of every
converted man, and the present possession of everyone
who is wholly sanctified by the baptism with the Holy
Ghost.

2. *Power over the flesh.* The body which God intended
for a ' house beautiful ' for the soul, and a temple holy
unto Himself, is often reduced to a sty, where the
imprisoned soul wallows in lusts and passions, and
degrades itself below the level of beasts. But this
baptism gives a man power over his body.

God has given to man such desires and passions as are
necessary to secure his continued existence. Not one is
in itself evil, but good and only good; and when con-
trolled and used, but not abused, will help to develop
and maintain the purest and highest manhood. The
appetites for food and drink are necessary to life. Another
desire is intended to secure the continuance of the human
race. And so all the desires and appetites of the body
have useful ends, and were given to us in love by our
heavenly Father for high and essential purposes, and are
necessary to us as human beings.

But the soul, cut off from fellowship with God by sin,
seeks satisfaction in sensual excesses and the unlawful
gratification of these appetites, and so sinks to depths of
degradation to which no beast ever falls. Thus man
becomes a slave; swollen and raging passion takes the
place of innocent appetites and desires.

Now, when the Holy Spirit enters the heart and

sanctifies the soul, He does not destroy these desires, but purifies and regulates them. He reinforces the soul with the fear and love of God, and gives it power, complete power, over the fleshly appetites. He restores it to its full fellowship with God and its kingship over the body.

But while these appetites and desires are not in themselves sinful, but are necessary for our welfare and our complete manhood, and while their diseased and abnormal power is cured when we are sanctified, they are still avenues through which we may be tempted. Therefore, they must be guarded with care and ruled in wisdom. Many people stumble at and reject the doctrine of entire sanctification because they do not understand these things. They mistake that which is natural and essential to a human being, for the diseased and abnormal propensity caused by sin, and so miss the blessed truth of full salvation.

I knew a doctor, who had used tobacco for over sixty years, delivered from the abnormal appetite instantly through sanctification of the Spirit. I knew an old man, who had been a drunkard for over fifty years, similarly delivered. I knew a young man, the slave of a vicious habit of the flesh, who was set free at once by the fiery baptism. The electric current cannot transform the dead wire into a live one quicker than the Holy Spirit can flood a soul with light and love, destroy the carnal mind, and fill a man with power over all sin.

3. *Power over the devil.* The indwelling presence of the Holy Spirit destroys all doubt as to the personality of the devil. He is discerned, and his malice is felt and known as never before.

In the dark a man may be so skilfully attacked that his enemy is not discovered, but not in the day. Many people in these days deny that there is any devil, only evil; but they are in the dark, so much in the dark that they not only say that there is no devil, but that there is no personal God, only good. But the day comes with the Holy Spirit's entrance, and then God is intimately known and the devil is discovered. And as he assailed Jesus after His baptism with the Spirit, so he does today all who receive the Holy Ghost. He comes as an angel of light to deceive, and as a roaring lion to devour and overcome with fear; but the soul filled with the Spirit outwits the devil and, clad in the whole armour of God, overcomes the old enemy.

Power ' over all the power of the enemy ' (Luke x. 19) is God's purpose for all His children. Power to do the will of God patiently and effectively, with naturalness and ease, or to suffer the will of God with patience and good cheer, comes with this blessed baptism. It is power for service or sacrifice, according to God's will. Have you this power? If not, it is for you. Yield yourself fully to Christ just now, and if you ask in faith you shall receive.

' HAVE YE RECEIVED THE HOLY GHOST SINCE YE BELIEVED? '

CHAPTER VII

Trying the Spirits

' Ye shall receive power, after that the Holy Ghost is come upon you.'

THOSE who have not the Holy Spirit, or who do not heed Him, fall easily and naturally into formalism, substituting lifeless ceremonies, sacraments, genuflections and ritualistic performances for the free, glad, living worship inspired by the indwelling Spirit. They sing, but not from the heart. They say their prayers, but they do not really pray. ' I prayed last night, mother,' said a child. ' Why, my child, you pray every night!' replied the mother. ' No,' said the child, ' I only said prayers, but last night I really prayed.' And his face shone. He had opened his heart to the Holy Spirit, and had at last really talked with God and worshipped.

But those who receive the Holy Spirit may fall into fanaticism, unless they follow the command of John to ' try the spirits whether they are of God ' (1 John iv. 1).

We are commanded to ' despise not prophesyings ', but at the same time we are commanded to ' prove all things ' (1 Thess. v. 20, 21). ' Many false prophets are gone out into the world ' (1 John iv. 1) and, if possible, will lead us astray. So we must beware. As someone has written, we must ' believe not every spirit; regard not, trust not, follow not, every pretender to the Spirit of God, or every professor of vision, or inspiration or revelation from God '.

The higher and more intense the life, the more carefully must it be guarded, lest it be endangered and go astray. It is so in the natural world, and likewise in the spiritual world.

44

When Satan can no longer rock people to sleep with religious lullabies, or satisfy them with the lifeless form, then he comes as an angel of light, probably in the person of some professor or teacher of religion, and seeks to usurp the place of the Holy Spirit; but instead of leading ' into all truth ', he leads the unwary soul into deadly error; instead of directing him on to the highway of holiness, and into the path of perfect peace, where no ravenous beast ever comes, he leads him into a wilderness where the soul, stripped of its beautiful garments of salvation, is robbed and wounded and left to die, if some good Samaritan, with patient pity and Christlike love, come not that way.

1. When the Holy Spirit comes in His fullness, He strips men of their self-righteousness and pride and conceit. They see themselves as the chief of sinners, and realize that only through the stripes of Jesus are they healed; and ever after, as they live in the Spirit, their boast is in Him and their glory is in the Cross. Remembering the hole of the pit from which they were digged, they are filled with tender pity for all who are out of the way; yet, while they do not excuse or belittle sin, they are slow to believe evil, and their judgments are full of charity.

> Judge not; the workings of his brain
>   And of his heart thou canst not see;
> What looks to thy dim eyes a stain,
>   In God's pure light may only be
> A scar, brought from some well-won field,
> Where thou wouldst only faint and yield.

But the man who has been thus snared by Satan forgets his own past miserable state, boasts of his righteousness and thanks God that he was never as other men; he begins to beat his fellow-servants with heavy denunciations, thrust them through with sharp criticisms, and pelt them with hard words. He ceases to pity and begins to condemn; he no longer warns and entreats men in tender love, but is quick to believe evil, and swift to pass judgment, not only upon their actions, but upon their motives as well.

True charity has no fellowship with deeds of darkness. It never calls evil good, it does not wink at iniquity, but it is as far removed from this sharp, condemning spirit as light is from darkness, as honey is from vinegar. It is quick to condemn sin, but is full of saving, long-suffering compassion for the sinner.

2. A humble, teachable mind marks those in whom the Holy Spirit dwells. They esteem very highly in love those who are over them in the Lord, and are glad to be admonished by them. They submit themselves one to the other in the fear of the Lord, welcome instruction and correction, and esteem open rebuke better than secret love (Prov. xxvii. 5). They believe that the Lord has yet many things to say unto them, and they are willing and glad for Him to say them by whom He will, but especially by their leaders and their brethren. While they do not fawn and cringe before men, nor believe everything that is said to them, without proving it by the word and Spirit of God, they believe that God ' gave some, apostles; and some, prophets; and some, evangelists; and some, pastors and teachers; For the perfecting of the saints, for the work of the ministry, for the edifying of the body of Christ ' (Eph. iv. 11, 12); and, like Cornelius, they are ready to hear these appointed ministers, and receive the word of the Lord from them.

But Satan seeks to destroy all this lowliness of spirit and humbleness of mind. One in whom his deadly work has begun is ' wiser in his own conceit than seven men that can render a reason ' (Prov. xxvi. 16). He is wiser than all his teachers, and no man can instruct him. One of these deluded souls, who had previously been marked by modesty and humility, declared of certain of God's chosen leaders whose spiritual knowledge and wisdom were everywhere recognized, that ' the whole of them knew no more about the Holy Ghost than an old goose'. Paul, Luther and Wesley were much troubled, and their work greatly hurt, by some of these misguided souls, and every great spiritual awakening is likely to be marred more or less by such people; so that we cannot be too much on our guard against false spirits who would counterfeit the work and leadings of the Holy Spirit.

It is this huge conceit that has led some men to announce themselves as apostles and prophets to whom all men must listen, or fall under the wrath of God; while others have declared that they were living in resurrection bodies and should not die; and yet others have reached that pitch of fanaticism where they could calmly proclaim themselves to be the Messiah, or the Holy Ghost in bodily form. Such people will be quick to deny the infallibility of the Pope, while they assume their own infallibility and denounce all who dispute it.

The Holy Spirit may lead to a holy rivalry in love and humility and brotherly kindness and self-denial and good works, but He never leads men into the swelling conceit of such exclusive knowledge and superior wisdom that they can no longer be taught by their fellow-men.

3. Again, the man who is filled with the Spirit tolerates those who differ from him in opinion, in doctrine. He is firm in his own convictions, and ready at all times with meekness and fear to explain and defend the doctrines which he holds and is convinced are according to God's word, but he does not condemn and consign to damnation all those who differ from him. He is glad to believe that men are often better than their creed and may be saved in spite of it; that, like mountains whose bases are bathed with sunshine and clothed with fruitful fields and vineyards, while their tops are covered with dark clouds, so men's hearts are often fruitful in the graces of charity, while their heads are yet darkened by doctrinal error.

Anyway, as ' the servant of the Lord ', he will ' not strive; but be gentle unto all men, apt to teach, patient, In meekness instructing those that oppose themselves;

if God peradventure will give them repentance to the acknowledging of the truth; And that they may recover themselves out of the snare of the devil' (2 Tim. ii. 24-26).

But when Satan comes as an angel of light he will, under guise of love for and loyalty to the truth, introduce the spirit of intolerance. It was this spirit that crucified Jesus; that burned Huss and Cranmer at the stake; that hanged Savonarola; that inspired the massacre of Bartholomew and the horrors of the Inquisition; and it is the same spirit, in a milder but possibly more subtle form, that blinds the eyes of many professing Christians to any good in those who differ from them in doctrine, forms of worship or methods of government. They murder love to protect what they often blindly call truth. What is truth without love? A dead thing, an encumbrance, the letter that killeth!

The body is necessary to our life in this world, but life can exist in a deformed and even mutilated body; and such a body with life in it is better than the most perfect body that is only a corpse. So, while truth is most precious, and sound doctrine to be esteemed more than silver and gold, love can exist where truth is not held in its most perfect and complete forms, and love is the one thing needful.

> For the love of God is broader
> Than the measure of man's mind;
> And the heart of the Eternal
> Is most wonderfully kind.

4. The Holy Ghost begets a spirit of unity among Christians. People who have been sitting behind their sectarian fences in self-complacent ease, or proud indifference, or proselytizing zeal, or grim defiance, are suddenly lifted above the fence, and find sweet fellowship with each other, when He comes into their hearts.

They delight in each other's society; they each esteem others better than themselves, and in honour they prefer one another before themselves. They fulfil the

Psalmist's ideal: ' Behold, how good and how pleasant it is for brethren to dwell together in unity! ' (cxxxiii. 1). Here is a picture of the unity of Christians in the beginning in Jerusalem: ' And they were all filled with the Holy Ghost, and they spake the word of God with boldness. And the multitude of them that believed were of one heart and of one soul: neither said any of them that ought of the things which he possessed was his own; but they had all things common ' (Acts iv. 31, 32). What an ideal is this! And since it has been attained once, it can be attained again and retained, but only by the indwelling of the Holy Ghost. It was for this that Jesus poured out His heart in His great intercessory prayer, recorded in John xvii., just before His arrest in the Garden of Gethsemane. He says, ' I pray for them. . . . Neither pray I for these alone, but for them also which shall believe on Me through their word; That they all may be one.' And what was the standard of unity to which He would have us come? Listen!

' As Thou, Father, art in Me, and I in Thee, that they also may be one in Us: that the world may believe that Thou hast sent Me.' Such unity has a wondrous power to compel the belief of worldly men. ' And the glory which Thou gavest Me I have given them; that they may be one, even as We are one: I in them, and Thou in Me, that they may be made perfect in one; and that the world may know that Thou hast sent Me, and hast loved them, as Thou hast loved Me ' (verses 9, 20-23). Wondrous unity! Wondrous love!

It is for this His blessed heart eternally yearns, and it is for this that the Holy Spirit works in the hearts of those who receive Him. But Satan ever seeks to destroy this holy love and divine unity. When he comes, he arouses suspicions, he stirs up strife, he quenches the spirit of intercessory prayer, he engenders backbitings and causes separations.

After enumerating various Christian graces, and urging the Colossians to put them on, Paul adds: 'And

above all these things put on charity (or love), which is
the bond of perfectness' (Col. iii. 14). These graces
were garments, and love was the girdle which bound
and held them together; and so love is the bond that
holds true Christians together.

Divine love is the great test by which we are to try
ourselves and all teachers and spirits.

Love is not puffed up. Love is not bigoted. Love is
not intolerant. Love is not schismatic. Love is loyal
to Jesus and to all His people. If we have this love shed
abroad in our hearts by the Holy Ghost, we shall discern
the voice of our Good Shepherd, and we shall not be
deceived by the voice of the stranger; and so we shall be
saved from both formalism and fanaticism.

'HAVE YE RECEIVED THE HOLY GHOST SINCE YE
BELIEVED?'

CHAPTER VIII

Guidance

' Ye shall receive power, after that the Holy Ghost is come upon you.'

IT is the work of the Holy Spirit to guide the people of God through the uncertainties and dangers and duties of this life to their home in Heaven. When He led the children of Israel out of Egypt, by the hand of Moses, He guided them through the waste, mountainous wilderness, in a pillar of cloud by day and of fire by night, thus assuring their comfort and safety. And this was but a type of His perpetual spiritual guidance of His people.

' But how may I certainly know what God wants of me? ' is sure to become the earnest and, oftentimes, the agonizing cry of every humble and devoutly zealous young Christian. ' How may I know the guidance of the Holy Spirit? ' is asked again and again.

1. It is well for us to get it fixed in our minds that we need to be guided always by Him. A ship was wrecked on a rocky coast far out of the course that the captain thought he was taking. On examination, it was found that the compass had been slightly deflected by a bit of metal that had lodged in the box.

But the voyage of life on which we each one sail is beset by as many dangers as the ship at sea; and how shall we surely steer our course to our heavenly harbour without divine guidance? There is a wellnigh infinite number of influences to deflect us from the safe and certain course. We start out in the morning, and we know not what person we may meet, what paragraph we may read, what word may be spoken, what letter we may receive, what subtle temptation may assail or allure us, what immediate decisions we may have to make during the day, that may turn us almost imperceptibly, but none the less surely, from the right way. We need the guidance of the Holy Spirit.

2. We not only need divine guidance, but we may have it. God's word assures us of this. Oh! how my heart was comforted and assured one morning by these words: 'And the Lord shall guide thee continually' (Isa. lviii. 11). Not occasionally, not spasmodically, but 'continually'. Hallelujah! The Psalmist says: 'This God is our God for ever and ever: He will be our guide even unto death' (xlviii. 14). Jesus said of the Holy Spirit: 'Howbeit when He, the Spirit of truth, is come, He will guide you into all truth' (John xvi. 13). And Paul wrote: 'As many as are led by the Spirit of God, they are the sons of God' (Rom. viii. 14).

These Scriptures establish the fact that the children of God may be guided always by the Spirit of God.

> Guide me, O Thou great Jehovah,
>   Pilgrim through this barren land;
> I am weak, but Thou art mighty;
>   Hold me with Thy powerful hand.

3. How does God guide us?

(a) Paul says, 'We walk by faith, not by sight' (2 Cor. v. 7) and, 'The just shall live by faith' (Rom. i. 17). So we may conclude that the guidance of the Holy Spirit is such as still to demand the exercise of faith. God never leads us in such a way as to do away with the necessity of faith. When God warned Noah, we read that it was by faith that Noah was led to build the ark. When God told Abraham to go to a land which He would show him, it was by faith that Abraham went (Heb. xi. 7, 8). If we believe, we shall surely be guided; but if we do not believe, we shall be left to ourselves. Without faith it is impossible to please God (Heb. xi. 6), or to follow where He leads.

(b) The Psalmist says, 'The meek will He guide in

judgment' (xxv. 9). From this we gather that the Spirit guides us in such manner as to demand the exercise of our best judgment. He enlightens our understanding and directs our judgment by sound reason and sense.

I knew a man who was eager to obey God and to be led by the Spirit, but who had the mistaken idea that the Holy Spirit sets aside human judgment and common sense, and speaks directly upon the most minute and commonplace matters. He wanted the Holy Spirit to direct him just how much to eat at each meal; and he has been known to take food out of his mouth at what he supposed to be the Holy Spirit's notification that he had eaten enough, and that if he swallowed that mouthful it would be in violation of the leadings of the Spirit.

No doubt the Spirit will help an honest man to arrive at a safe judgment even in matters of this kind, but it will doubtless be through the use of his sanctified common sense. Otherwise, he is reduced to a state of mental infancy and kept in intellectual swaddling clothes. He will guide us in judgment; but it is only as we resolutely, and in the best light we have, exercise judgment.

(c) John Wesley said that God usually guided him by presenting reasons to his mind for any given course of action.

The Psalmist says, ' Thou shalt guide me with Thy counsel ' (lxxiii. 24) and ' I will instruct thee and teach thee in the way which thou shalt go ' (xxxii. 8). Now, counsel, instruction and teaching not only imply effort upon the part of the teacher, but also study and close attention on the part of the one being taught. Thus this guidance of the Holy Spirit will require us to listen attentively, study diligently and learn patiently the lessons He would teach us; and we see that the Holy Spirit does not set aside our powers and faculties, but seeks to awaken and stir them into full activity, and develop them into well-rounded perfection, thus making them channels through which He can intelligently influence and direct us.

What he seeks to do is to illuminate our whole spiritual being, as the sun illuminates our physical being, and bring us into such union and sympathy, such oneness of thought, desire, affection and purpose with God, that we shall, by a kind of spiritual instinct, know at all times the mind of God concerning us, and never be in doubt about His will.

4. The Holy Spirit guides us:

(a) By opening up to our minds the deep, sanctifying truths of the Bible, and especially by revealing to us the character and spirit of Jesus and His apostles, and leading us to follow in their footsteps—the footsteps of their faith and love and unselfish devotion to God and man, even unto the laying down of their lives.

(b) By the circumstances and surroundings of our daily life.

(c) By the counsel of others, especially of devout and wise and experienced men and women of God.

(d) By deep inward conviction, which increases as we wait upon Him in prayer and readiness to obey. It is by this sovereign conviction that men are called to preach, to go to foreign fields as missionaries, to devote their time, talents, money and lives to God's work for the bodies and souls of men.

5. Why do people seek for guidance and not find it?

(a) Because they do not diligently study God's word and seek to be filled with its truths and principles. They neglect the cultivation of their minds and hearts in the school of Christ, and so miss divine guidance. One of the mightiest men of God now living used to carry his Bible with him into the coal mine when only a boy, and spent his spare time filling his mind and heart with its heavenly truths, and so prepared himself to be divinely led in mighty labours for God.

(b) They do not humbly accept the daily providences, the circumstances and conditions of their everyday life as a part of God's present plan for them; as His school in which He would train them for greater things; as His vineyard in which He would have them diligently labour.

A young woman imagined she was called to devote herself entirely to saving souls; but under the searching training through which she had to pass saw her selfishness, and she said she would have to return home and live a holy life there, and seek to get her family saved—something which she had utterly neglected—before she could go into the work. If we are not faithful at home, or in the shop, or mill, or store where we work, we shall miss God's way for us.

(c) Because they are not teachable, and are unwilling to receive instruction from other Christians. They are not humble-minded.

(d) Because they do not wait on God and listen and heed the inner leadings of the Holy Spirit. They are self-willed; they want their own way. Someone has said, ' That which is often asked of God is not so much His will and way, as His approval of our way.' And another has said, ' God's guidance is plain, when we are true.' If we promptly and gladly obey we shall not miss the way. Paul said of himself, ' I was not disobedient unto the heavenly vision ' (Acts xxvi. 19). He obeyed God at all costs, and so the Holy Spirit could guide him.

(e) Because of fear and unbelief. It was this fearfulness of unbelief that caused the Israelites to turn back and not go into Canaan, when Caleb and Joshua assured them that God would help them to possess the land. They lost sight of God and feared the giants and walled cities, and so missed God's way for them and perished in the wilderness.

(f) Because they do not take everything promptly and confidently to God in prayer.

Paul tells us to be ' instant in prayer' (Rom. xii, 12) ; and I am persuaded that it is slowness and delay to pray, and sloth and sleepiness in prayer, that rob God's children of the glad assurance of His guidance in all things.

(g) Because of impatience and haste. Some of God's plans for us unfold slowly; and we must patiently and calmly wait on Him in faith and faithfulness, assured that in due time He will make plain His way for us, if our faith fail not. It is never God's will that we should get into a headlong hurry; but that, with patient steadfastness, we should learn to stand still when the pillar of cloud and fire does not move, and that with loving confidence and glad promptness we should strike our tents and march forward when He leads.

> When we cannot see our way,
> Let us trust and still obey;
> He who bids us forward go,
> Cannot fail the way to show.
>
> Though the sea be deep and wide,
> Though a passage seem denied,
> Fearless let us still proceed,
> Since the Lord vouchsafes to lead.

Finally, we may rest assured that the Holy Spirit never leads His people to do anything that is wrong, or that is contrary to the will of God as revealed in the Bible. He never leads anyone to be impolite and discourteous. 'Be courteous' (1 Pet. iii. 8) is a divine command. He would have us respect the minor graces of gentle, kindly manners, as well as the great laws of holiness and righteousness.

He may sometimes lead us in ways that are hard for flesh and blood, and that bring to us sorrow and loss in this life. He led Jesus into the wilderness to be sore tried by the devil, and to Pilate's judgment hall, and to the Cross. He led Paul in ways that meant imprisonment, stonings, whippings, hunger and cold, and bitter persecution and death. But He upheld Paul until he cried out, 'Most gladly . . . will I rather glory in my infirmities, that the power of Christ may rest upon me.

Therefore I take pleasure in infirmities, in reproaches, in necessities, in persecutions, in distresses for Christ's sake ' (2 Cor. xii. 9, 10). Hallelujah! Oh, to be thus led by our heavenly Guide!

> He leadeth me! O blessèd thought!
> O words with heavenly comfort fraught!
> Whate'er I do, where'er I be,
> Still 'tis God's hand that leadeth me.
>
> Sometimes 'mid scenes of deepest gloom,
> Sometimes where Eden's bowers bloom,
> By waters still, o'er troubled sea,
> Still 'tis His hand that leadeth me.
>
> Lord, I would clasp Thy hand in mine,
> Nor ever murmur or repine,
> Content, whatever lot I see,
> Since 'tis my God that leadeth me.
>
> And when my task on earth is done,
> When by Thy grace the victory's won,
> E'en death's cold wave I will not flee,
> Since God through Jordan leadeth me.

' HAVE YE RECEIVED THE HOLY GHOST SINCE YE BELIEVED ? '

CHAPTER IX

The Meek and Lowly Heart

' Ye shall receive power, after that the Holy Ghost is come upon you.'

I KNOW a man whose daily prayer for years was that he might be meek and lowly in heart as was his Master. 'Take My yoke upon you, and learn of Me,' said Jesus; 'for I am meek and lowly in heart' (Matt. xi. 29).

How lowly Jesus was! He was the Lord of life and glory. He made the worlds and upholds them by His word of power (John i., Heb. i.). But He humbled Himself and became man, and was born of the Virgin in a manger among the cattle. He lived among the common people and worked at the carpenter's bench. And then, anointed with the Holy Spirit, He went about doing good, preaching the gospel to the poor, and ministering to the manifold needs of the sick and sinful and sorrowing. He touched the lepers; He was the Friend of publicans and sinners. His whole life was a ministry of mercy to those who most needed Him. He humbled Himself to our low estate. He was a King who came 'lowly, and riding upon an ass, and upon a colt the foal of an ass' (Zech. ix. 9). He was a King, but His crown was of thorns, and a Cross was His throne.

What a picture Paul gives us of the mind and heart of Jesus! He exhorts the Philippians, saying, ' Let nothing be done through strife or vainglory; but in lowliness of mind let each esteem other better than themselves '; and then he adds, ' Let this mind be in you, which was also in Christ Jesus: Who, being in the form of God, thought it not robbery to be equal with God: But made Himself of no reputation, and took upon

Him the form of a servant, and was made in the likeness
of men: And being found in fashion as a man, He
humbled Himself, and became obedient unto death,
even the death of the cross ' (ii. 3-8).

Now, when the Holy Spirit finds His way into the
heart of a man, the Spirit of Jesus has come to that man,
and leads him to the same meekness of heart and lowly
service that were seen in the Master.

Ambition for place and power and money and fame
vanishes, and in its place is a consuming desire to be good
and do good, to accomplish in full the blessed, the
beneficent will of God.

Some time ago I met a woman who, as a trained
nurse in Paris, nursing rich, English-speaking foreigners,
received pay that in a few years would have made her
independently wealthy; but the spirit of Jesus came into
her heart, and she is now nursing the poor, giving her
life to them, and doing for them service the most loathsome and exacting, and doing it with a smiling face, for
her food and clothes.

Some able men in one of our largest American cities
lost their spiritual balance, cut themselves loose from all
other Christians, and made for a time quite a religious
stir among many good people. They were very clear and
powerful in their presentation of certain phases of truth,
but they were also very strong, if not bitter, in their
denunciations of all existing religious organizations. They
attacked the churches and The Salvation Army, pointing
out what they considered wrong so skilfully and with
such professions of sanctity, that many people were made
most dissatisfied with the churches and with the Army.

An Army Captain listened to them, and was greatly
moved by their fervour, their burning appeals, their
religious ecstasy, and their denunciations of the luke-
warmness of other Christians, including the Army. She
began to wonder if after all they were not right, and
whether or not the Holy Spirit was amongst us. Her
heart was full of distress, and she cried to God. And then

the vision of our slum (now Goodwill) officers rose before her eyes. She saw their devotion, their sacrifice, their lowly, hidden service, year after year, among the poor and ignorant and vicious, and she said to herself, ' Is not this the Spirit of Jesus ? Would these men, who denounce us so, be willing to forgo their religious ecstasies and spend their lives in such lowly, unheralded service ? ' And the mists that had begun to blind her eyes were swept away, and she saw Jesus still amongst us going about doing good in the person of our slum officers and of all who for His name's sake sacrifice their time and money and strength to bless and save their fellow-men.

You who have visions of glory and rapturous delight, and so count yourselves filled with the Spirit, do these visions lead you to virtue and to lowly, loving service? If not, take heed to yourselves, lest, exalted like Capernaum to Heaven, you are at last cast down to Hell. Thank God for the mounts of transfiguration where we behold His glory! But down below in the valley are children possessed of devils; and to them He would have us go with the glory of the mount on our faces, and lowly love and vigorous faith on our hearts, and clean hands ready for any service. He would have us give ourselves to them; and if we love Him, if we follow Him, if we are truly filled with the Holy Spirit, we will.

A Captain used to slip out of bed early in the morning to pray, and then black his own and his Lieutenant's boots. God mightily blessed him. Recently I saw him, now a Commissioner, with thousands of officers and soldiers under his command, at an outing in the woods by the lake shore, looking after poor and forgotten soldiers, and giving them food with his own hand. Like the Lord, his eyes seemed to be in every place beholding opportunities to do good, and his feet and hands always followed his eyes; and this is the fruit of the indwelling Holy Spirit.

' HAVE YE RECEIVED THE HOLY GHOST SINCE YE BELIEVED ? '

CHAPTER X

Hope

' Ye shall receive power, after that the Holy Ghost is come upon you.'

ARE you ever cast down and depressed in spirit?
Listen to Paul: ' Now the God of hope fill you
with all joy and peace in believing, that ye may
abound in hope, through the power of the Holy Ghost '
(Rom. xv. 13). What cheer is in those words! They ring
like the shout of a triumph.

God Himself is ' the God of hope '. There is no
gloom, no depression, no wasting sickness of deferred
hope in Him. He is a brimming fountain and ocean
of hope eternally, and He is our God. He is our hope.

Out of His infinite fullness He is to fill us; not half
fill us, but fill us with joy, ' all joy ', hallelujah! ' and
peace '.

And this is not by some condition or means that is so
high and difficult that we cannot perform our part, but
it is simply ' in believing '—something which the little
child or the aged philosopher, the poor man and the
rich man, the ignorant and the learned can do. And
the result will be abounding ' hope, through the power of
the Holy Ghost '.

And what power is that? If it is physical power,
then the power of a million Niagaras and flowing
oceans and rushing worlds is as nothing compared to it.
If it is mental power, then the power of Plato and Bacon
and Milton and Shakespeare and Newton is as the light
of a fire-fly to the sun when compared to it. If it is
spiritual power, then there is nothing with which it can
be compared. But suppose it is all three in one, infinite

and eternal! This is the power, throbbing with love and mercy, to which we are to bring our little hearts by living faith; and God will fill us with joy and peace and hope by the incoming of the Holy Spirit.

God's people are a hopeful people. They hope in God, with whom there is no change, no weakness, no decay. In the darkest night and the fiercest storm they still hope in Him, though it may be feebly. But He would have His people ' abound in hope ' so that they should always be buoyant, triumphant.

But how can this be in a world such as this? We are surrounded by awful, mysterious and merciless forces that at any moment may overwhelm us. The fire may burn us, the water may drown us, the hurricane may sweep us away, friends may desert us, foes may master us. There is the depression that comes from failing health, from poverty, from overwork and sleepless nights and constant care, from thwarted plans, disappointed ambitions, slighted love and base ingratitude. Old age comes on with its grey hairs, failing strength, dimness of sight, dullness of hearing, tottering step, shortness of breath and general weakness and decay. The friends of youth die, and a new, strange, pushing generation that knows not the old man, comes elbowing him aside and taking his place. Under some blessed outpouring of the Spirit the work of God revives, vile sinners are saved, Zion puts on her beautiful garments, reforms of all kind advance, the desert blossoms as the rose, the waste place becomes a fruitful field, and the millennium seems just at hand. Then the spiritual tide recedes, the forces of evil are emboldened, they mass themselves and again sweep over the heritage of the Lord, leaving it waste and desolate; and the battle must be fought over again.

How can one be always hopeful, always abounding in hope, in such a world? Well, hallelujah! it is possible ' through the power of the Holy Ghost ', but only through His power; and this power will not fail so long as we fix our eyes on eternal things and believe.

The Holy Spirit, dwelling within, turns our eyes from that which is temporal to that which is eternal; from the trial itself to God's purpose in the trial; from the present pain to the precious promise.

I am now writing in a little city made rich by vast potteries. If the dull, heavy clay on the potter's wheel and in the fiery oven could think and speak, it would doubtless cry out against the fierce agony; but if it could foresee the purpose of the potter and the thing of use and beauty he meant to make it, it would nestle low under his hand and rejoice in hope.

We are clay in the hand of the divine Potter, but we can think and speak, and in some measure understand His high purpose in us. It is the work of the Holy Spirit to make us understand. And if we will not be dull and senseless and unbelieving, He will illuminate us and fill us with peaceful, joyous hope.

1. He would reveal to us that our heavenly Potter has Himself been on the wheel and in the fiery furnace, learning obedience and being fashioned into ' the Captain of our salvation ' by the things which He suffered. When we are tempted and tried, and tempest-tossed, He raises our hope by showing us Jesus suffering and sympathizing with us, tempted in all points as we are, and so able and wise and willing to help us in our struggle and conflict (Heb. ii. 9-18). He assures us that Jesus, into whose hands is committed all power in Heaven and earth, is our elder Brother, ' touched with the feeling of our infirmities ' (Heb. iv. 15), and He encourages us to rest in Him and not be afraid; and so we abound in hope through His power, as we believe.

2. He reveals to us the eternal purpose of God in our trials and difficulties. Listen to Paul: ' All things work together for good to them that love God.' ' We know,' says Paul (Rom. viii. 28). But how can this be? Ah! there is where faith must be exercised. It is ' in believing ' that we ' abound in hope, through the power of the Holy Ghost ' (Rom. xv. 13).

God's wisdom and ability to make all things work together for our good are not to be measured by our understanding, but to be firmly held by our faith. My child is in serious difficulty and does not know how to help himself; but I say, ' Leave it to me '. He may not understand how I am to help him, but he trusts me and rejoices in hope. We are God's dear children, and He knows how to help us and make all things work together for our good, if we will only commit ourselves to Him in faith.

> Thou art as much His care as if beside
> Nor man nor angel lived in Heaven or earth;
> Thus sunbeams pour alike their glorious tide
> To light up worlds, or wake an insect's mirth.

Again, when afflictions overtake us, the Holy Spirit encourages our hope and makes it to abound by many promises. ' Our light affliction, which is but for a moment, worketh for us a far more exceeding and eternal weight of glory; While we look not at the things which are seen, but at the things which are not seen: for the things which are seen are temporal; but the things which are not seen are eternal ' (2 Cor. iv. 17, 18). But such a promise as that only mocks us if we do not believe. ' In all their affliction He was afflicted, and the angel of His presence saved them: in His love and in His pity He redeemed them; and He bare them, and carried them all the days of old ' (Isa. lxiii. 9). And He is just the same today. To some He says: ' I have chosen thee in the furnace of affliction ' (Isa. xlviii. 10) and, nestling down into His will and ' believing ', they ' abound in hope, through the power of the Holy Ghost '.

He turns our eyes back upon Job in his loss and pain; upon Joseph sold into Egyptian slavery; Daniel in the lions' den; the three Hebrews in the burning fiery furnace, and Paul in prison and shipwreck and manifold perils; and, showing us their steadfastness and their final triumph, He prompts us to hope in God.

When weakness of body overtakes us, He encourages

us with such assurances as these: ' My flesh and my heart
faileth: but God is the strength of my heart, and my
portion for ever ' (Ps. lxxiii. 26); and the words of
Paul, ' Though our outward man perish, yet the inward
man is renewed day by day ' (2 Cor. iv. 16).

When old age comes creeping on apace, we can rely
on His promise to meet the need, that our hope fail not.
The Psalmist prays: ' Cast me not off in the time of
old age; forsake me not when my strength faileth. . . .
Now also when I am old and greyheaded, O God,
forsake me not; until I have shewed Thy strength unto
this generation, and Thy power to every one that is
to come ' (Ps. lxxi. 9, 18). And in Isaiah the Lord
replies: ' Even to your old age I am He; and even to
hoar hairs will I carry you: I have made, and I will bear;
even I will carry, and will deliver you ' (Isa. xlvi. 4).
And the Psalmist cries out: ' The righteous shall flourish
like the palm tree: he shall grow like a cedar in Lebanon.
Those that be planted in the house of the Lord shall
flourish in the courts of our God. They shall still bring
forth fruit in old age; they shall be fat and flourishing;
To shew that the Lord is upright ' (Ps. xcii. 12-15).

These are sample promises of which the Bible is full,
and which have been adapted by infinite wisdom and
love to meet us at every point of doubt and fear and
need, that, in believing them, we may have a steadfast
and glad hope in God. He is pledged to help us. He
says: ' Fear thou not; for I am with thee: be not dis-
mayed; for I am thy God: I will strengthen thee; yea,
I will help thee; yea, I will uphold thee with the right
hand of My righteousness ' (Isa. xli. 10).

When all God's waves and billows swept the
Psalmist, and his soul was bowed within him, he cried
out: ' Why art thou cast down, O my soul? and why
art thou disquieted in me? hope thou in God: for
I shall yet praise Him for the help of His countenance '
(Ps. xlii. 5). And Jeremiah, remembering the worm-
wood and the gall, and the deep mire of the dungeon

into which they had plunged him, and from which he had scarcely been delivered, said: ' It is good that a man should both hope and quietly wait for the salvation of the Lord ' (Lam. iii. 26).

When the Holy Spirit is come, He brings to remembrance these precious promises and makes them living words; and, if we believe, the whole heaven of our soul shall be lighted up with abounding hope. Hallelujah! It is only through ignorance of God's promises, or through weak and wavering faith, that hope is dimmed. Oh, that we may heed the still small voice of the heavenly Comforter, and steadfastly, joyously believe!

> My hope is built on nothing less
> Than Jesus' Blood and righteousness . . .
>
> When all around my soul gives way,
> He then is all my hope and stay.

' HAVE YE RECEIVED THE HOLY GHOST SINCE YE BELIEVED ? '

CHAPTER XI

The Holy Spirit's Substitute for Gossip and Evil-speaking

' Ye shall receive power, after that the Holy Ghost is come upon you.'

THE other day I heard a man of God say, ' We cannot bridle the tongues of the people among whom we live: they will talk '; and by talk he meant gossip and criticism and fault-finding.

> You never can tell when you send a word—
>> Like an arrow shot from a bow
> By an archer blind—be it cruel or kind,
>> Just where it will chance to go.
> It may pierce the breast of your dearest friend,
>> Tipped with its poison or balm;
> To a stranger's heart in life's great mart
>> It may carry its pain or its calm.

The wise mother, when she finds her little boy playing with a sharp knife, or the looking-glass, or some dainty dish, does not snatch it away with a slap on his cheek or harsh words, but quietly and gently substitutes a safer and more interesting toy, and so avoids a storm.

A sensible father who finds his boy reading a book of dangerous tendency, will kindly point out its character and substitute a better book that is equally interesting.

When children want to spend their evenings on the street, thoughtful and intelligent parents will seek to make their evenings at home more healthfully attractive.

When a man seeks to rid his mind of evil and hurtful thoughts, he will find it wise to follow Paul's exhortation to the Philippians: ' Brethren, whatsoever things are true . . . honest . . . just . . . pure . . . lovely . . . of good report . . . if there be any praise, think on these things ' (Phil. iv. 8).

Any man who faithfully, patiently and persistently accepts this programme of Paul's, will find his evil thoughts vanishing away.

And this is the Holy Spirit's method. He has a pleasant and safe substitute for gossip and fault-finding and slander.

Here it is: ' Be filled with the Spirit; Speaking to yourselves in psalms and hymns and spiritual songs, singing and making melody in your heart to the Lord; Giving thanks always for all things unto God and the Father in the name of our Lord Jesus Christ ' (Eph. v. 18-20). This is certainly a fruit of being filled with the Spirit.

Many years ago the Lord gave me a blessed revival in a little village in which nearly every soul in the place, as well as farmers from the surrounding country, were converted. One result was that they now had no time for gossip and doubtful talk about their neighbours. They were all talking about religion and rejoicing in the things of the Lord. If they met each other on the street, or in some shop or store, they praised the Lord, and encouraged each other to press on in the heavenly way. If they met a sinner, they tenderly besought him to be reconciled to God, to give up his sins, ' flee from the wrath to come ', and start at once for Heaven. If they met in each other's houses, they gathered around the organ or the piano and sang hymns and songs, and did not part till they had united in prayer.

There was no criticizing of their neighbours, no grumbling and complaining about the weather, no fault-finding with their lot in life, or their daily surroundings and circumstances. Their conversation was joyous, cheerful, and helpful to one another. Nor was it forced and out of place, but rather it was the natural, spontaneous outflow of loving, humble, glad hearts filled with the Spirit, in union with Jesus, and in love and sympathy with their fellow-men.

And this is, I think, our heavenly Father's ideal of

social and spiritual intercourse for His children on earth. He would not have us separate ourselves from each other and shut ourselves up in convents and monasteries in austere asceticism on the one hand, nor would He have us light and foolish, or fault-finding and censorious on the other hand, but sociable, cheerful, and full of tender, considerate love.

On the day of Pentecost, when they were all filled with the Holy Ghost and a multitude were converted, we read that ' they, continuing daily with one accord in the temple, and breaking bread from house to house, did eat their meat with gladness and singleness of heart, Praising God, and having favour with all the people' (Acts ii. 46,47). This is a sample of the brotherly love and unity which our heavenly Father would have throughout the whole earth; but how the breath of gossip and evil-speaking would have marred this heavenly fellowship and separated these ' chief friends '!

> Lord, subdue our selfish will;
>   Each to each our tempers suit
> By Thy modulating skill,
>   Heart to heart, as lute to lute.

Let no one suppose, however, that the Holy Spirit accomplishes this heavenly work by some overwhelming baptism which does away with the need of our co-operation. He does not override us, but works with us; and we must intelligently and determinedly work with Him in this matter.

People often fall into idle and hurtful gossip and evil-speaking, not so much from ill-will as from old habit, as a wagon falls into a rut; or they drift into it with the current of conversation about them; or they are beguiled into it by a desire to say something, and be pleasant and entertaining.

But when the Holy Spirit comes He lifts us out of the old ruts, and we must follow Him with care lest we fall into them again, possibly never more to escape. He gives us life and power to stem the adverse currents about us, but we must exercise ourselves not to be swept downward by them. He does not destroy the desire to please, but He subordinates it to the desire to help and bless, and we must stir ourselves up to do this.

When Miss Havergal was asked to sing and play before a worldly company, she sang a sweet song about Jesus and, without displeasing anybody, greatly blessed the company.

At a breakfast party John Fletcher told his experience so sweetly and naturally that all hearts were stirred, the Holy Ghost fell upon the company, and they ended with a glorious prayer meeting.

William Bramwell used at meals to turn the conversation into spiritual channels to the blessing of all who were present, so that they had two meals—one for the body and one for the soul.

To do this wisely and helpfully requires thought and prayer and a fixed purpose, and a tender, loving heart filled with the Holy Spirit.

I know a mother who seeks to have a brief season of prayer and a text of Scripture just before going to dinner to prepare her heart to guide the conversation along spiritual highways.

Are you careful and have you victory in this matter, my comrade? If not, seek it just now in simple, trustful prayer, and the Lord who loves you will surely answer, and will be your helper from this time forth. He surely will. Believe just now, and henceforth ' let your conversation be as it becometh the gospel of Christ ' (Phil. i. 27).

> I ask Thee, ever blessed Lord,
> That I may never speak a word
> Of envy born, or passion stirred.
>
> First, true to Thee in heart and mind,
> Then always to my neighbour kind,
> By Thy good hand to good inclined.
>
> O save from words that bear a sting,
> That pain to any brother bring;
> Inbreathe Thy calm in everything.

Let love within my heart prevail,
To rule my words when thoughts assail,
That, hid in Thee, I may not fail.

I know, my Lord, Thy power within
Can save from all the power of sin;
In Thee let every word begin.

Should I be silent? Keep me still,
Glad waiting on my Master's will;
Thy message through my lips fulfil.

Give me Thy words when I should speak,
For words of Thine are never weak,
But break the proud, but raise the meek.

Into Thy lips all grace is poured,
Speak Thou through me, eternal Word,
Of thought, of heart, of lips the Lord.

' HAVE YE RECEIVED THE HOLY GHOST SINCE YE
BELIEVED ? '

CHAPTER XII

The Sin Against the Holy Ghost

' Ye shall receive power, after that the Holy Ghost is come upon you.'

GOD is love, and the Holy Spirit is ceaselessly striving to make this love known in our hearts, work out God's purposes of love in our lives, and transform our character by love. And so we are solemnly warned against resisting the Spirit, and almost tearfully and always tenderly exhorted to ' quench not the Spirit ' (1 Thess. v. 19), and to ' grieve not the holy Spirit of God, whereby ye are sealed unto the day of redemption ' (Eph. iv. 30).

There is one great sin against which Jesus warned the Jews, as a sin never to be forgiven in this world nor in that which is to come. That was blasphemy against the Holy Ghost.

That there is such a sin, Jesus teaches in Matt. xii. 31, 32; Mark iii. 28-30; and Luke xii. 10. And it may be that this is the sin referred to in Heb. vi. 4-6; x. 29.

Since many of God's dear children have fallen into dreadful distress through fear that they had committed this sin, it may be helpful for us to study carefully as to what constitutes it.

Jesus was casting out devils, and Mark tells us that ' the scribes which came down from Jerusalem said, He hath Beelzebub, and by the prince of the devils casteth He out devils '. To this Jesus replied with gracious kindness and searching logic: ' How can Satan cast out Satan? And if a kingdom be divided against itself, that kingdom cannot stand. And if a house be divided against itself, that house cannot stand. And if

72

Satan rise up against himself, and be divided, he cannot stand, but hath an end. No man can enter into a strong man's house, and spoil his goods, except he will first bind the strong man; and then he will spoil his house.'

In this quiet reply we see that Jesus does not rail against them, nor flatly deny their base assertion that He does His miracles by the power of the devil, but shows how logically false must be their statement. And then, with grave authority and, I think, with solemn tenderness in His voice and in His eyes, He adds, ' Verily I say unto you, All sins shall be forgiven unto the sons of men, and blasphemies wherewith soever they shall blaspheme: But he that shall blaspheme against the Holy Ghost hath never forgiveness, but is in danger of eternal damnation '; or, as the Revised Version has it, ' is guilty of an eternal sin '; and then Mark adds, ' Because they said, He hath an unclean spirit ' (Mark iii. 22-30).

Jesus came into the world to reveal God's truth and love to men, and to save them; and men are saved by believing in Him. But how could the men of His day, who saw Him working at the carpenter's bench, and living the life of an ordinary man of humble toil and daily temptation and trial, believe His stupendous claim to be the only-begotten Son of God, the Saviour of the world, and the final Judge of all men? Any wilful and proud impostor could make such a claim. But men *could* not and *ought* not to believe such an assertion unless the claim were supported by ungainsayable evidence. This evidence Jesus began to give, not only in the holy life which He lived and the pure gospel He preached, but in the miracles He wrought, the blind eyes He opened, the sick He healed, the hungry thousands He fed, the seas He stilled, the dead He raised to life again, and the devils He cast out of bound and harassed souls.

The Scribes and Pharisees witnessed these miracles, and were compelled to admit these signs and wonders. Nicodemus, one of their number, said to Jesus, ' Rabbi, we know that Thou art a teacher come from God: for no man can do these miracles that Thou doest, except God be with him ' (John iii. 2). Would they now admit His claim to be the Son of God, their promised and long-looked-for Messiah? They were thoughtful men and very religious, but not spiritual. The gospel He preached was Spirit and life; it appealed to their conscience and revealed their sin, and to acknowledge Him was to admit that they themselves were wrong. It meant submission to His authority, the surrender of their wills, and a change of front in their whole inner and outer life. This meant moral and spiritual revolution in each man's heart and life; and to this they would not submit. And so to avoid such plain inconsistency, they must discredit His miracles; and since they could not deny them, they declared that He wrought them by the power of the devil.

Jesus worked these signs and wonders by the power of the Holy Spirit, that He might win their confidence, and that they might reasonably believe and be saved. But they refused to believe, and in their malignant obstinacy heaped scorn upon Him, accusing Him of being in league with the devil; and how could they be saved? This was the sin against the Holy Spirit against which Jesus warned them. It was not so much one act of sin, as a deep-seated, stubborn rebellion against God that led them to choose darkness rather than light, and so to blaspheme against the Spirit of truth and light. It was sin full and ripe and ready for the harvest.

Someone has said that ' this sin cannot be forgiven, not because God is unwilling to forgive, but because one who thus sins against the Holy Spirit has put himself where no power can soften his heart or change his nature. A man may misuse his eyes and yet see; but whosoever puts them out can never see again. One may misdirect his compass, and turn it aside from the North Pole by a magnet or piece of iron, and it may recover and point right again; but whosoever destroys the compass itself has lost his guide at sea '.

Many of God's dear children, honest souls, have been persuaded that they have committed this awful sin. Indeed, I once thought that I myself had done so, and for twenty-eight days I felt that, like Jonah, I was ' in the belly of hell '. But God, in love and tender mercy, drew me out of the horrible pit of doubt and fear, and showed me that this is a sin committed only by those who, in spite of all evidence, harden their hearts in unbelief, and to shield themselves in their sins deny and blaspheme the Lord.

Dr. Daniel Steele tells of a Jew who was asked, ' Is it that you *cannot*, or that you *will not* believe? ' The Jew passionately replied, ' We *will* not, we *will* not believe.'

This was wilful refusal and rejection of light, and in that direction lies hardness of heart beyond recovery, fullness of sin, and final impenitence, which are unpardonable.

Doubtless many through resistance to the Holy Spirit come to this awful state of heart; but those troubled, anxious souls who think they have committed this sin are not usually among the number.

An Army officer in Canada was in the midst of a glorious revival, when one night a gentleman arose and, with deep emotion, urged the young people present to yield themselves to God, accept Jesus as their Saviour and receive the Holy Spirit. He told them that he had once been a Christian, but that he had not walked in the light and, consequently, had sinned against the Holy Spirit, and could never more be pardoned. Then, with all earnest tenderness, he exhorted them to be warned by his sad state, and not to harden their hearts against the gracious influences, and entreated them to yield to the Saviour. Suddenly the scales of doubt dropped from his eyes, and he saw that he had not in his inmost heart rejected Jesus; that he had not committed the unpardonable sin—

> For the love of God is broader
> Than the measure of man's mind;
> And the heart of the Eternal
> Is most wonderfully kind.

And in an instant his heart was filled with light and love and peace, and sweet assurance that Christ Jesus was his Saviour, even his.

In one meeting, I have known three people who thought they had committed this sin, and were bowed with grief and fear, to come to the Penitent-form and find deliverance.

The poet Cowper was plunged into unutterable gloom by the conviction that he had committed this awful sin; but God tenderly brought him into the light and sweet comforts of the Holy Spirit again, and doubtless it was in the sense of such lovingkindness that he wrote:

> There is a fountain filled with Blood,
>   Drawn from Immanuel's veins;
> And sinners plunged beneath that flood
>   Lose all their guilty stains.

John Bunyan was also afflicted with horrible fears that he had committed the unpardonable sin, and in his little book entitled, *Grace Abounding to the Chief of Sinners* (a book which I would earnestly recommend to all soul-winners), he tells how he was delivered from his doubts and fears and was filled once more with the joy of the Lord. There are portions of his *Pilgrim's Progress* which are to be interpreted in the light of this grievous experience.

Those who think they have committed this sin may generally be assured that they have not.

1. Their hearts are usually very tender, while this sin must harden the heart past all feeling.

2. They are full of sorrow and shame for having neglected God's grace and trifled with the Saviour's dying words, but such sorrow could not exist in a heart so fully given over to sin that pardon was impossible.

3. God says, ' Whosoever will may come '; and if they find it in their hearts to come, they will not be cast out, but freely pardoned and received with loving-kindness through the merits of Jesus' Blood. God's promise will not fail; His faithfulness is established in

the heavens. Bless His holy name! Those who have committed this sin are full of evil, and do not care to come; they will not and, therefore, are never pardoned. Their sin is eternal.

'HAVE YE RECEIVED THE HOLY GHOST SINCE YE BELIEVED?'

CHAPTER XIII

Offences Against the Holy Ghost

' Ye shall receive power, after that the Holy Ghost is come upon you.'

ONE day, in a fit of boyish temper, I spoke hot words of anger, somewhat unjustly, against another person, and this deeply grieved my mother. She said but little, and though her sweet face has mouldered many years beneath the Southern daisies, her look of grief I can still see across the years of a third of a century. That is the one sad memory of my childhood. A stranger might have been amused or incensed at my words, but mother was grieved—grieved to her heart by my lack of generous, self-forgetful, thoughtful love.

We can anger a stranger or an enemy, but it is only a friend we grieve. The Holy Spirit is such a Friend, more tender and faithful than a mother; and shall we carelessly offend Him, and estrange ourselves from Him in spite of His love?

There is a sense in which every sin is against the Holy Ghost. Of course, not every such sin is unpardonable, but the tendency of all sin is in that direction, and we are only safe as we avoid the very beginnings of sin. Only as we ' walk in the Spirit ' are we ' free from the law of sin and death ' (Rom. viii. 2). Therefore, it is infinitely important that we beware of offences against the Spirit, ' lest any of you be hardened through the deceitfulness of sin ' (Heb. iii. 13).

Grieving the Holy Spirit is a very common and a very sad offence of professing Christians, and it is to this that must be attributed much of the weakness and ignorance and joylessness of so many followers of Christ.

And He is grieved, as was my mother, by the unloving speech and spirit of God's children.

In his letters to the Ephesians, Paul says, ' Let no corrupt communication proceed out of your mouth, but that which is good to the use of edifying, that it may minister grace unto the hearers.' And then he adds: ' And grieve not the holy Spirit of God, whereby ye are sealed unto the day of redemption. Let all bitterness, and wrath, and anger, and clamour, and evil-speaking, be put away from you, with all malice: And be ye kind one to another, tenderhearted, forgiving one another, even as God for Christ's sake hath forgiven you. Be ye therefore followers of God, as dear children; and walk in love, as Christ also hath loved us, and hath given Himself for us ' (Eph. iv. 29-v. 2).

What does Paul teach us here? That it is not by some huge wickedness, some Judas-like betrayal, some tempting and lying to the Holy Ghost, as did Ananias and Sapphira (Acts v. 1-10), that we grieve Him, but by that which most people count little and unimportant; by talk that corrupts instead of blessing and building up those that hear, by gossip, by bitterness, and uncharitable criticisms and fault-findings. This was the sin of the elder son when the prodigal returned, and it was by this he pierced with grief the kind old father's heart.

By getting in a rage, by loud, angry talking and evil-speaking and petty malice, by unkindness and hard-heartedness and an unforgiving spirit, we grieve Him. In a word, by not walking through the world as in our Father's house, and among our neighbours and friends as among His dear children; by not loving tenderly and making kindly sacrifices for one another, He is grieved. And this is not a matter of little importance. It may have sadly momentous consequences.

It is a bitter, cruel and often irreparable thing to trifle with a valuable earthly friendship. How much more when the friendship is heavenly; when the friend is our Lord and Saviour, our Creator and Redeemer, our Governor and Judge, our Teacher, Guide and God! When we trifle with a friend's wishes—especially when such wishes are all in perfect harmony with and for our highest possible good—we may not estrange the friend from us, but we estrange ourselves from our friend. Our hearts grow cold toward him, though his heart may be breaking with longing toward us.

The more Saul ill-treated David, the more he hated David.

Such estrangement may lead, little by little, to yet greater sin, to strange hardness of heart, to doubts and unbelief, and backslidings and denial of the Lord.

The cure for all this is a clean heart full of sweet and gentle, self-forgetful, generous love. Then we shall be ' followers of God, as dear children ', then we shall ' walk in love, as Christ also hath loved us, and hath given Himself for us ' (Eph. v. 1, 2).

But there is another offence, that of quenching the Spirit, which accounts for the comparative darkness and deadness of many of God's children.

In 1 Thess. v. 16-19 the Apostle says: ' Rejoice evermore. Pray without ceasing. In every thing give thanks: for this is the will of God in Christ Jesus concerning you. Quench not the Spirit.'

When will the Lord's dear children learn that the religion of Jesus is a lowly thing, and that it is the little foxes that spoil the vines? Does not the Apostle here teach that it is not by some desperate, dastardly deed that we quench the Spirit, but simply by neglecting to rejoice and pray, and give thanks at all times and for all things?

It is not necessary to blot the sun out of the heavens to keep the sunlight out of your house—just close the blinds and draw the curtains; nor do you pour barrels of water on the flames to quench the fire—just shut off the draught; nor do you dynamite the city reservoir and destroy all the mains and pipes to cut off your supply of sparkling water, but just refrain from turning on the tap.

So you do not need to do some great evil, some deadly

sin, to quench the Spirit. Just cease to rejoice, through fear of man and of being peculiar; be prim and proper as a white and polished gravestone; let gushing joy be curbed; neglect to pray when you feel a gentle pull in your heart to get alone with the Lord; omit giving hearty thanks for all God's tender mercies, faithful discipline and loving chastenings, and soon you will find the Spirit quenched. He will no longer spring up joyously like a well of living water within you.

But give the Spirit a vent, an opening, a chance, and He will rise within you and flood your soul with light and love and joy.

Some years ago a sanctified woman of clear experience went alone to keep her daily hour with God; but, to her surprise, it seemed that she could not find Him, either in prayer or in His word. She searched her heart for evidence of sin, but the Spirit showed her nothing contrary to God in her mind, heart or will. She searched her memory for any breach of covenant, any broken vows, any neglect, any omission, but could find none.

Then she asked the Lord to show her if there were any duty unfulfilled, any command unnoticed, which she might perform, and quick as thought came the words, ' Rejoice evermore. Have you done that this morning? '

She had not. It had been a busy morning, and a well-spent one, but so far there had been no definite rejoicing in her heart, though the manifold riches and ground for joy of all Christians were hers.

At once she began to count her blessings and thank the Lord for each one, and rejoice in Him for all the way He had led her, and the gifts He had bestowed, and in a very few minutes the Lord stood revealed to her spiritual consciousness.

She had not committed sin, nor resisted the Spirit, but a failure to rejoice in Him who had daily loaded her with benefits (Ps. lxviii. 19) had in a measure quenched the Spirit. She had not turned on the main, and so her soul was not flooded with living waters. She had not remembered the command: ' Thou shalt rejoice before the Lord thy God in all that thou puttest thine hands unto' (Deut. xii. 18). But that morning she learned a lifelong lesson, and she has ever since safeguarded her soul by obeying the many commands to ' rejoice in the Lord '.

Grieving and quenching the Spirit will not only leave barren and desolate an individual soul, but it will do so for a corps, a church, a community, a whole nation or continent. We see this illustrated on a large scale by the long and weary Dark Ages, when the light of the gospel was almost extinguished, and only here and there was the darkness broken by the torch of truth held aloft by some humble, suffering soul that had wept and prayed, and through painful struggles had found the light.

We see it also in those corps, churches, communities and countries where revivals are unknown, or are a thing of the past, where souls are not born into the Kingdom, and where there is no joyous shout of victory among the people of God.

Grieving and quenching the Spirit may be done unintentionally by lack of thought and prayer and hearty devotion to the Lord Jesus; but they prepare the way and lead to intentional and positive resistance to the Spirit.

To resist the Spirit is to fight against Him.

The sinner who, listening to the gospel invitation, and convicted of sin, refuses to submit to God in true repentance and faith in Jesus, is resisting the Holy Spirit.

We have bold and striking historical illustrations of the danger of resisting the Holy Spirit in the disasters which befell Pharaoh, which came upon Jerusalem, and have for twenty centuries followed the Jews.

The ten plagues that came upon Pharaoh and his people were ten opportunities and open doors into God's favour and fellowship, which they themselves shut by their stubborn resistance, only to be overtaken by dreadful catastrophe.

To the Jews, Stephen said, ' Ye do always resist the

Holy Ghost ' (Acts vii. 51); and the siege and fall of Jerusalem, and the butchery and enslavement of its inhabitants, and all the woes that came upon the Jews, followed their rejection of Jesus and the hardness of heart and spiritual blindness which swiftly overtook them when they resisted all the loving efforts and entreaties of His disciples baptized with the Holy Spirit.

And what on a large scale befalls nations and people, on a small scale also befalls individuals. Those that receive and obey the Lord are enlightened and blessed and saved; those that resist and reject Him are sadly left to themselves and surely swallowed up in destruction.

Likewise the professing Christian who hears of heart-holiness and cleansing from all sin as a blessing he may now have by faith and, convicted of his need of the blessing and of God's desire and willingness to bestow it upon him now, refuses to seek it in whole-hearted affectionate consecration and faith, is resisting the Holy Spirit. And such resistance imperils the soul beyond all possible computation.

We see an example of this in the Israelites who were brought out of Egypt with signs and wonders, and led through the Red Sea and the wilderness to the borders of Canaan, but, forgetting, refused to go over into the land. In this they resisted the Holy Spirit in His lead-ings as surely as did Pharaoh, and with quite as disastrous results to themselves, perishing in their evil way.

For their sin was as much greater than his as their light exceeded his.

Hundreds of years later, a prophet, writing of this time, says: ' In all their affliction He was afflicted, and the angel of His presence saved them: in His love and in His pity He redeemed them; and He bare them, and carried them all the days of old. But they rebelled, and vexed His Holy Spirit: therefore He was turned to be their enemy, and He fought against them ' (Isa. lxiii. 9, 10).

We see from this that Christians must beware and

watch and pray and walk softly with the Lord in glad obedience and childlike faith, if they would escape the darkness and dryness that result from grieving and quenching the spirit, and the dangers that surely come from resisting Him.

> Arm me with jealous care,
>   As in Thy sight to live ;
> And O Thy servant, Lord prepare
>   A strict account to give !
>
> Help me to watch and pray,
>   And on Thyself rely,
> Assured, if I my trust betray,
>   I shall for ever die.

'HAVE YE RECEIVED THE HOLY GHOST SINCE YE BELIEVED?'

CHAPTER XIV

The Holy Spirit and Sound Doctrine

' Ye shall receive power, after that the Holy Ghost is come upon you.'

IS Jesus Christ divine? Is the Bible an inspired Book? Is man a fallen creature who can be saved only through the suffering and sacrifice of the Creator? Will there be a resurrection of the dead, and a day in which God will judge all the world by the Man Christ Jesus? Is Satan a personal being, and is there a Hell in which the wicked will be for ever punished?

These are great doctrines which have been held and taught by His followers since the days of Jesus and His apostles, and yet they are ever being attacked and denied.

Are they true? Or are they only fancies and falsehoods, or figures of speech and distortions of truth? How can we find truth and know it?

Jesus said, ' When He, the Spirit of truth, is come, He will guide you into all truth ' (John xvi. 13).

What truth? Not the truth of the multiplication table, or of physical science, or art, or secular history, but spiritual truth—the truth about God and His will and character, and our relations to Him in Christ, that truth which is necessary to salvation and holiness—into all this truth the Holy Spirit will guide us. ' He shall teach you all things,' said Jesus (John xiv. 26).

How, then, shall we escape error and be ' sound in doctrine '? Only by the help of the Holy Spirit.

How do we know Jesus Christ is divine? Because the Bible tells us so? Infinitely precious and important is this revelation in the Bible; but not by this do we know it. Because the church teaches it in her creed, and we have heard it from the catechism? Nothing taught in any creed or catechism is of more vital importance; but neither by this do we know it.

How then? Listen to Paul: 'No man can say that Jesus is the Lord, but by the Holy Ghost' (1 Cor. xii. 3). 'No man,' says Paul. Then learning it from the Bible or catechism is not to know it except as the parrot might know it; but every man is to be taught this by the Holy Spirit, if he is really to know it.

Then it is not a revelation made once for all, and only to the men who walked and talked with Jesus, but it is a spiritual revelation made anew to each believing heart that in penitence seeks Him and so meets the conditions of such a revelation.

Then the poor, degraded, ignorant outcast at the Army Penitent-form in the slums of London or Chicago who never heard of a creed, and the ebony African and dusky Indian who never saw the inside of a Bible, may have Christ revealed in him, and know by the revelation of the Holy Spirit that Jesus is Lord.

'It pleased God . . . to reveal His Son in me,' wrote Paul (Gal. i. 15, 16); and again, ' Christ liveth in me ' (Gal. ii. 20); and again, ' My little children, of whom I travail in birth again until Christ be formed in you ' (Gal. iv. 19); as though Christ is to be spiritually formed in the heart of each believer by the operation of the Holy Spirit, as He was physically formed in the womb of Mary by the same Spirit (Luke i. 35); and again, ' The mystery which hath been hid from ages and from generations, but now is made manifest to His saints . . . which is Christ in you, the hope of glory ' (Col. i. 26, 27); ' That Christ may dwell in your hearts by faith ' (Eph. iii. 17); ' Examine yourselves, whether ye be in the faith; prove your own selves. Know ye not your own selves, how that Jesus Christ is in you, except ye be reprobates ' (2 Cor. xiii. 5).

' At that day,' said Jesus, when making His great promise of the Comforter to His disciples, ' At that day ye shall know that I am in My Father, and ye in Me, and I in you ' (John xiv. 20); and again, in His great prayer, He said: ' I have declared unto them Thy name, and will declare it: that the love wherewith Thou hast loved Me may be in them, and I in them ' (John xvii. 26).

It is this ever-recurring revelation to penitent, believing hearts, by the agency of the ever-present Holy Spirit, that makes faith in Jesus Christ living and invincible. ' I know He is Lord, for He saves my soul from sin, and He saves me now ', is an argument that rationalism and unbelief cannot answer nor overthrow; and so long as there are men in the world who can say this, faith in the divinity of Jesus Christ is secure; and this experience and witness come by the Holy Ghost.

> I worship Thee, O Holy Ghost,
> I love to worship Thee;
> My risen Lord for aye were lost
> But for Thy company.

And so it is by the guidance and teaching of the Holy Spirit that all saving truth becomes vital to us.

It is He that makes the Bible a living book; it is He that convinces the world of judgment (John xvi. 8-11); it is He that makes men certain that there is a Heaven of surpassing and enduring glory and joy, and a Hell of endless sorrow and woe for those who sin away their day of grace and die in impenitence.

Who have been the mightiest and most faithful preachers of the gloom and terror and pain of a perpetual Hell? Those who have been the mightiest and most effective preachers of God's compassionate love.

In all periods of great revival, when men seemed to live on the borderland, and in the vision of eternity, Hell has been preached. The leaders in these revivals have been men of prayer and faith and consuming love, but they have been men who knew ' the terrors of the Lord ' and, therefore, they preached the judgments of God, and they proved that the law with its penalties is a schoolmaster to bring men to Christ (Gal. iii. 24). Fox, the Quaker; Bunyan, the Baptist; Baxter, the Puritan; Wesley and Fletcher, and Whitefield and Caughey, the Methodists; Finney, the Presbyterian; Edwards and Moody, the Congregationalists; and General Booth, the Salvationist; all have preached it, not savagely, but tenderly and faithfully, as a mother might warn her child against some great danger that would surely follow careless and selfish wrong-doing.

What men have loved and laboured and sacrificed as these men? Their hearts have been a flaming furnace of love and devotion to God, and an over-flowing fountain of love and compassion for men; but just in proportion as they have discovered God's love and pity for the sinner, so have they discovered His wrath against sin and all obstinate wrong-doing; and as they have caught glimpses of Heaven and declared its joys and everlasting glories to men, so they have seen Hell, with its endless punishment, and with trembling voice and over-flowing eyes have they warned men to ' flee from the wrath to come '.

Were these men, throbbing with spiritual life and consumed with devotion to the Kingdom of God and the everlasting well-being of their fellow-men, led to this belief by the Spirit of Truth, or were they misled?

' The things of the Spirit of God . . . are spiritually discerned ' (1 Cor. ii. 14), says Paul. It is not by searching and philosophizing that these things are found out, but by revelation. ' Flesh and blood hath not revealed it unto thee,' said Jesus to Peter, ' but My Father which is in Heaven ' (Matt. xvi. 17). The great teacher of truth is the Spirit of Truth, and the only safe expounders and guardians of sound doctrine are men filled with the Holy Ghost.

Study and research have their place, and an important place; but in spiritual things they will be of no avail unless prosecuted by spiritual men. As well might men blind from birth attempt to study the starry heavens, and men born deaf undertake to expound and criticize the harmonies of Bach and Beethoven. Men must see and hear to speak and write intelligently on such subjects. And so men must be spiritually enlightened to understand spiritual truth.

The greatest danger to any religious organization is that a body of men should arise in its ranks, and hold its positions of trust, who have learned its great fundamental doctrines by rote out of the catechism, but have no experimental knowledge of their truth inwrought by the mighty anointing of the Holy Ghost, and who are destitute of ' an unction from the Holy One ', by which, says John, ' ye know all things ' (1 John ii. 20, 27).

Why do men deny the divinity of Jesus Christ? Because they have never placed themselves in that relation to the Spirit, and met those unchanging conditions that would enable Him to reveal Jesus to them as Saviour and Lord.

Why do men dispute the inspiration of the Scriptures? Because the Holy Ghost, who inspired ' holy men of God ' to write the book (2 Pet. i. 21), hides its spiritual sense from unspiritual and unholy men.

Why do men doubt a Day of Judgment, and a state of everlasting doom? Because they have never been bowed and broken and crushed beneath the weight of their sin, and by a sense of guilt and separation from a holy God that can only be removed by faith in His dying Son.

A sportsman lost his way in a pitiless storm on a black and starless night. Suddenly his horse drew back and refused to take another step. He urged it forward, but it only threw itself back upon its haunches. Just then a vivid flash of lightning revealed a great precipice upon the brink of which he stood. It was but an instant, and then the pitchy blackness hid it again from view. But he turned his horse and anxiously rode away from the terrible danger.

A distinguished professor of religion said to me some

time ago, ' I dislike, I abhor, the doctrine of Hell '; and
then after a while added, ' But three times in my life I
have seen that there was eternal separation from God
and an everlasting Hell for me, if I walked not in the
way God was calling me to go.'

Into the blackness of the sinner's night the Holy
Spirit, who is patiently and compassionately seeking the
salvation of all men, flashes a light that gives him a
glimpse of eternal things which, if heeded, would lead to
the sweet peace and security of eternal day.   For when
the Holy Spirit is heeded and honoured, the night passes,
the shadows flee away, the day dawns, the Sun of
righteousness arises with healing in His wings (Mal. iv. 2)
and, saved and sanctified, men walk in His light in
safety and joy.   Doctrines which before were repellent
to the carnal mind, and but foolishness or a stumbling-
block to the heart of unbelief, now become precious and
satisfying to the soul; and truths which before were hid
in impenetrable darkness, or seen only as through dense
gloom and fog, are now seen clearly as in the light of
broad day.

> Hold thou the faith that Christ is Lord,
>   God over all, who died and rose
> And everlasting life bestows
>   On all who hear the living word;
> For thee His life-blood He out-poured,
>   His Spirit sets thy spirit free;
> Hold thou the faith—He dwells in thee,
>   And thou in Him, and Christ is Lord!

' HAVE YE RECEIVED THE HOLY GHOST SINCE YE
BELIEVED ? '

CHAPTER XV

Praying in the Spirit

' Ye shall receive power, after that the Holy Ghost is come upon you.'

A N important work of the Holy Spirit is to teach us
how to pray, to instruct us what to pray for, and
to inspire us to pray earnestly, without ceasing and
in faith, for the things we desire and the things that are
dear to the heart of the Lord.

In a familiar verse, the poet Montgomery says:

> Prayer is the burden of a sigh,
> The falling of a tear,
> The upward glancing of an eye
> When none but God is near.

And no doubt he is right. Prayer is exceedingly
simple. The faintest cry for help, a whisper for mercy, is
prayer. But when the Holy Spirit comes and fills the
soul with His blessed presence, prayer becomes more
than a cry; it ceases to be a feeble request, and often
becomes a strife (Rom. xv. 30; Col. iv. 12) for greater
things, a conflict, an invincible argument, a wrestling
with God, and through it men enter into the divine
councils and rise into a blessed and responsible fellowship
in some important sense with the Father and the Son
in the moral government of the world.

It was in this spirit and fellowship that Abraham prayed
for Sodom (Gen. xviii. 23-32); that Moses interceded for
Israel, and stood between them and God's hot dis-
pleasure (Exod. xxxii. 7-14); and that Elijah prevailed
to shut up the heavens for three years and six months,
and then again prevailed in his prayer for rain (Jas. v.
17, 18).

God would have us come to Him not only as a foolish

and ignorant child comes, but as an ambassador to his home government; as a full-grown son who has become of age and entered into partnership with his father; as a bride who is one in all interests and affections with the bridegroom.

He would have us ' come boldly unto the throne of grace ' with a well-reasoned and scriptural understanding of what we desire, and with a purpose to ' ask ', ' seek ' and ' knock ' till we get the thing we wish, being assured that it is according to His will; and this boldness is not inconsistent with the profoundest humility and a sense of utter dependence; indeed, it is always accompanied by self-distrust and humble reliance upon the merits of Jesus, else it is but presumption and unsanctified conceit. This union of assurance and humility, of boldness and dependence, can be secured only by the baptism with the Holy Spirit, and only so can one be prepared and fitted for such prayer.

Three great obstacles hinder mighty prayer: selfishness, unbelief, and the darkness of ignorance and foolishness. The baptism with the Spirit sweeps away these obstacles and brings in the three great essentials to prayer: faith, love (divine love), and the light of heavenly knowledge and wisdom.

1. Selfishness must be cast out by the incoming of love. The ambassador must not be seeking personal ends, but the interests of his government and the people he represents; the son must not be seeking private gain, but the common prosperity of the partnership in which he will fully and lawfully share; the bride must not forget him to whom she belongs, and seek separate ends, but in all ways identify herself with her husband and his interests. So the child of God must come in prayer, unselfishly.

It is the work of the Holy Spirit, with our co-operation and glad consent, to search and destroy selfishness out of our hearts, and fill them with pure love to God and man. And when this is done we shall not then be asking for things amiss to consume them upon our lusts, to gratify our appetites, pride, ambition, ease or vain-glory. We shall seek only the glory of our Lord and the common good of our fellow-men, in which, as co-workers and partners, we shall have a common share. If we ask for success, it is not that we may be exalted, but that God may be glorified; that Jesus may secure the purchase of His Blood; that men may be saved, and the Kingdom of Heaven be established upon earth.

If we ask for daily bread, it is not that we may be full, but that we may be fitted for daily duty. If we ask for health, it is not alone that we may be free from pain and filled with physical comfort, but that we may be spent ' in publishing the sinner's Friend ', in fulfilling the work for which God has placed us here.

2. Unbelief must be destroyed. Doubt paralyses prayer. Unbelief quenches the spirit of intercession. Only as the eye of faith sees our Father God upon the throne guaranteeing to us rights and privileges by the Blood of His Son, and inviting us to come without fear and make our wants known, does prayer rise from the commonplace to the sublime; does it cease to be a feeble, timid cry, and become a mighty spiritual force, moving God Himself in the interests which it seeks.

Men, wise with the wisdom of this world, but poor and naked and blind and foolish in matters of faith, ask: ' Will God change His plans at the request of man? ' And we answer, ' Yes,' since many of God's plans are made contingent upon the prayers of His people, and He has ordered that prayer offered in faith, according to His will, revealed in His word, shall be one of the controlling factors in His government of men.

Is it God's will that the tides of the Atlantic and Pacific should sweep across the Isthmus of Panama? That men should run under the Alps? That thoughts and words should be winged across the ocean without any visible or tangible medium? Yes; it is His will, if men will it, and work to these ends in harmony with His great physical laws. So in the spiritual world there are wonders wrought by prayer, and God wills the will of His people when they come to Him in faith and love.

What else is meant by such promises and assurances as these: ' Therefore I say unto you, What things soever ye desire, when ye pray, believe that ye receive them, and ye shall have them ' (Mark xi. 24) ; ' The supplication of a righteous man availeth much in its working. Elijah was a man of like passions with us, and he prayed fervently that it might not rain; and it rained not on the earth for three years and six months. And he prayed again; and the heavens gave rain, and the earth brought forth her fruit ' (Jas. v. 16-18. R.V.).

The Holy Spirit dwelling within the heart helps us to understand the things we may pray for, and the heart that is full of love and loyalty to God only wants what is lawful. This is mystery to people who are under the dominion of selfishness and the darkness of unbelief, but it is a soul-thrilling fact to those who are filled with the Holy Ghost.

' What wilt thou that I shall do unto thee ? ' asked Jesus of the blind man (Luke xviii. 41). He had respect to the will of the blind man, and granted his request, seeing he had faith. And Jesus still has respect to the vigorous sanctified will of His people—the will that has been subdued by consecration and faith into loving union with His will.

The Lord answered Abraham on behalf of Sodom till he ceased to ask.

' The Lord has had His way so long with Hudson Taylor,' said a friend, ' that now Hudson Taylor can have his way with the Lord.'

Adoniram Judson lay sick with a fatal illness in far-away Burma. His wife read to him an account of the conversion of a number of Jews in Constantinople through some of his writings. For a while the sick man was silent, and then he spoke with awe, telling his wife that for years he had prayed that he might be used in some way to bless the Jews, yet never having seen any evidence that his prayers were answered; but now, after many years and from far away, the evidence of answer had come. Then, after further silence, he spoke with deep emotion, saying that he had never prayed a prayer for the glory of God and the good of men but that, sooner or later, even though for the time being he had forgotten, he found that God had not forgotten, but had remembered and patiently worked to answer his prayer.

Oh, the faithfulness of God! He means it when He makes promises and exhorts and urges and commands us to pray. It is not His purpose to mock us, but to answer and ' to do exceeding abundantly above all that we ask or think ' (Eph. iii. 20). Bless His holy name!

3. Knowledge and wisdom must take the place of foolish ignorance. Paul says, ' We know not what we should pray for as we ought '; and then adds, ' but the Spirit itself maketh intercession for us with groanings which cannot be uttered ' (Rom. viii. 26). If my little child asks for a glittering razor, I refuse its request; but when my full-grown son asks for one I grant it. So God cannot wisely answer some prayers, for they are foolish or untimely. Hence, we need not love and faith only, but wisdom and knowledge, that we may ask according to the will of God.

It is this that Paul has in mind when he says that he will not only pray with the Spirit, but ' I will pray with the understanding also ' (1 Cor. xiv. 15). Men should think before they pray, and study that they may pray wisely.

Now, when the Holy Spirit comes there pours into the soul not only a tide of love and simple faith, but a flood of light as well, and prayer becomes not only earnest, but intelligent also. And this intelligence increases as, under the leadership of the Holy Spirit, the word of God is studied, and its heavenly truths and principles are grasped and assimilated.

It is thus men come to know God and become His friends, whose prayers He will assist and will not deny.

Such men talk with God as friend with Friend, and the Holy Spirit helps their infirmities; encourages them to urge their prayer in faith; teaches them to reason with God; enables them to come boldly in the name of Jesus, when oppressed with a sense of their own insignificance and unworthiness; and, when words fail them and they scarcely know how to voice their desires, He intercedes within them with unutterable groanings, according to the will of God (Rom. viii. 26, 27).

A young man felt called to mission work in China, but his mother offered strong opposition to his going. An agent of the mission, knowing the need of the work and vexed with the mother, one day laid the case before Hudson Taylor.

> ' Mr. Taylor ', said he, ' listened patiently and lovingly to all I had to say, and then gently suggested our praying about it. Such a prayer I have never heard before! It seemed to me more like a conversation with a trusted friend whose advice he was seeking. He talked the matter over with the Friend from every point of view—from the side of the young man, from the side of China's needs, from the side of the mother, and her natural feelings, and also from my side. It was a revelation to me. I saw that prayer did not mean merely asking for things, much less asking for things to be carried out by God according to our ideas; but that it means *communion*, fellowship, partnership, with our heavenly Father. And when our will is really blended with His, what liberty we may have in asking for what we want! '

Hallelujah!

> My soul, ask what thou wilt,
> Thou canst not be too bold;
> Since His own Blood for thee He spilt,
> What else can He withhold?

' HAVE YE RECEIVED THE HOLY GHOST SINCE YE BELIEVED? '

CHAPTER XVI

Characteristics of the Anointed Preacher

' Ye shall receive power, after that the Holy Ghost is come upon you.'

SINCE God saves men by ' the foolishness of preach
ing ', the preacher has an infinitely important work,
and he must be fitted for it. But what can fit a man
for such sacred work? Not education alone, not knowledge of books, not gifts of speech, not winsome manners,
nor a magnetic voice, nor a commanding presence, but
only God. The preacher must be more than a man—
he must be a man plus the Holy Ghost.

Paul was such a man. He was full of the Holy Spirit,
and in studying his life and ministry we get a life-sized
portrait of an anointed preacher living, fighting, preaching, praying, suffering, triumphing and dying in the
power and light and glory of the indwelling Spirit.

In the second chapter of the First of Thessalonians he
gives us a picture of his character and ministry which
were formed and inspired by the Holy Spirit, a sample
of His workmanship, and an example for all gospel
preachers.

At Philippi Paul had been terribly beaten with stripes
on his bare back, and roughly thrust into the inner
dungeon, where his feet were made fast in the stocks; but
that did neither break nor quench his spirit. Love
burned in his heart, and his joy in the Lord brimmed
full and bubbled over; and at midnight, in the damp,
dark, loathsome dungeon, he and Silas, his comrade in
service and suffering, ' prayed, and sang praises unto
God '. God answered with an earthquake, and the
jailer and his household got gloriously converted. Paul
was set free and went at once to Thessalonica, where,

regardless of the shameful way he had been treated at Philippi, he preached the gospel boldly, and a blessed revival followed with many converts; but persecution arose, and Paul had again to flee. His heart, however, was continually turning back to these converts, and at last he sat down and wrote them this letter. From this we learn that:

1. He was a *joyful* preacher. He was no pessimist, croaking out doleful prophecies and lamentations and bitter criticisms. He was full of the joy of the Lord. It was not the joy that comes from good health, a pleasant home, plenty of money, wholesome food, numerous and smiling friends, and sunny, favouring skies; but a deep, springing fountain of solemn, gladdening joy that abounded and overflowed in pain and weariness, in filthy, noisome surroundings, in loneliness and poverty, danger and bitter persecutions. No earth-born trial could quench it, for it was Heaven-born; it was ' the joy of the Lord ' poured into his heart with the Holy Spirit.

2. He was a *bold* preacher. Worldly prudence would have constrained him to go softly at Thessalonica, after his experience at Philippi, lest he arouse opposition and meet again with personal violence; but, instead, he says, ' We were bold in our God to speak unto you the gospel of God with much contention ' (1 Thess. ii. 2). Personal considerations were all forgotten, or cast to the winds, in his impetuous desire to declare the gospel and save their souls. He lived in the will of God and conquered his fears. ' The wicked flee when no man pursueth: but the righteous are bold as a lion ' (Prov. xxviii. 1).

This boldness is a fruit of righteousness, and is always found in those who are full of the Holy Ghost. They forget themselves and so lose all fear. This was the secret of the martyrs when burned at the stake or thrown to the wild beasts.

Fear is a fruit of selfishness. Boldness thrives when selfishness is destroyed. God esteems it, commands His people to be courageous, and makes spiritual leaders only of those who possess courage (Joshua i. 9).

Moses feared not the wrath of the king, refused to be called the son of Pharaoh's daughter, and boldly espoused the cause of his despised and enslaved people.

Joshua was full of courage. Gideon fearlessly attacked one hundred and twenty thousand Midianites, with but three hundred unarmed men.

David faced the lion and the bear, and inspired all Israel by battling with and killing Goliath.

The prophets were men of the highest courage, who fearlessly rebuked kings and, at the risk of life and often at the cost of life, denounced popular sins, and called the people back to righteousness and the faithful service of God. These men feared God, thus losing the fear of man. They believed God and so obeyed Him, and were entrusted with His high missions and everlasting employments.

'Fear thou not; for I am with thee,' saith the Lord (Isa. xli. 10); and this Paul believed, and so says, 'We were bold in our God.' God was his high tower, his strength and unfailing defence, and so he was not afraid.

Paul's boldness toward man was a fruit of his boldness toward God, and that, in turn, was a fruit of his faith in Jesus as his High Priest, who had been touched with the feeling of his infirmities, and through whom he could come boldly unto the throne of grace and obtain mercy, and find grace to help in every time of need (Heb. iv. 16).

It is the timidity and delicacy with which men attempt God's work that often accounts for their failure. Let them speak out boldly like men, as ambassadors of Heaven, who are not afraid to represent their King, and they will command attention and respect and reach the hearts and consciences of men.

I have read that quaint old Bishop Latimer, who was afterward burned at the stake, 'having preached a sermon before King Henry VIII, which greatly displeased the monarch, was ordered to preach again on the next Sunday, and make apology for the offence given. The day came, and with it a crowded assembly anxious to hear the bishop's apology. Reading his text, he commenced thus: "Hugh Latimer, dost thou know before whom thou art this day to speak? To the high and mighty monarch, the king's most excellent majesty, who can take away thy life if thou offendest. Therefore, take heed that thou speakest not a word that may displease. But, then, consider well, Hugh, dost thou not know from whence thou comest? Upon whose message thou art sent? Even by the great and mighty God, who is all-present, and who beholdeth all thy ways, and who is able to cast thy soul into Hell! Therefore, take care that thou deliver thy message faithfully." '

He then repeated the sermon of the previous Sunday, word for word, but with double its former energy and emphasis. The Court was full of excitement to learn what would be the fate of this plain-dealing and fearless bishop. He was ordered into the king's presence, who, with a stern voice, asked, ' How dared you thus offend me?' 'I merely discharged my duty,' was Latimer's reply. The king arose from his seat, embraced the good man, saying, ' Blessed be God I have so honest a servant.'

He was a worthy successor of Nathan, who confronted King David with his sin, and said, ' Thou art the man.'

This divine courage will surely accompany the fiery baptism of the Spirit.

What is it but the indwelling of the Holy Spirit that gives courage to Salvation Army officers and soldiers, enabling them to face danger and difficulty and loneliness with joy, and attack sin in its worst forms as fearlessly as David attacked Goliath?

' Not by might, nor by power, but by My Spirit, saith the Lord ' (Zech. iv. 6).

> Shall I, for fear of feeble man,
> The Spirit's course in me restrain? . . .
>
> Awed by a mortal's frown, shall I
> Conceal the word of God most high? . . .

> Shall I, to soothe the unholy throng,
> Soften Thy truths and smooth my tongue? . . .

> How then before Thee shall I dare
> To stand, or how Thine anger bear? . . .

> Yea, let men rage, since Thou wilt spread
> Thy shadowing wings around my head;
> Since in all pain Thy tender love
> Will still my sure refreshment prove.

3. He was *without guile*. 'For our exhortation was not of deceit, nor of uncleanness, nor in guile: But as we were allowed of God to be put in trust with the gospel, even so we speak; not as pleasing men, but God, which trieth our hearts' (1 Thess. ii. 3, 4).

He was frank and open. He spoke right out of his heart. He was transparently simple and straightforward. Since God had honoured him with this infinite trust of preaching the gospel, he sought to preach it that he should please God regardless of men. And yet that is the surest way to please men. People who listen to such a man feel his honesty, and realize that he is seeking to do them good, to save them rather than to tickle their ears and win their applause, and in their hearts they are pleased.

But, anyway, whether or not they are pleased, he is to deliver his message as an ambassador and look to his home government for his reward. He gets his commission from God, and it is God who will try his heart and prove his ministry. Oh, to please Jesus! Oh, to stand perfect before God after preaching His gospel!

4. He was *not a time-server nor a covetous man*. 'Neither at any time used we flattering words, as ye know, nor a cloak of covetousness; God is witness,' he adds.

There are three ways of reaching a man's purse: (1) Directly. (2) By way of his head with flattering words. (3) By way of his heart with manly, honest, saving words. The first way is robbery. The second way is robbery, with the poison of a deadly, but pleasing, opiate added, which may damn his soul. The third reaches his purse by saving his soul and opening in his heart an unfailing fountain of benevolence to bless himself and the world.

It were better for a preacher to turn highwayman and rob men with a club and a strong hand, than, with smiles and smooth words and feigned and fawning affection, to rob them with flattery, while their poor souls, neglected and deceived, go down to Hell. How will he meet them in the Day of Judgment and look into their horror-stricken faces, realizing that he played and toyed with their fancies and affections and pride to get money and, instead of faithfully warning them and seeking to save them, with flattering words fattened their souls for destruction?

Not so did Paul. ' I seek not yours, but you,' he wrote the Corinthians. It was not their money, but their souls he wanted.

But such faithful love will be able to command all men have to give. Why, to some of his converts he wrote: ' I bear you record, that, if it had been possible, ye would have plucked out your own eyes, and have given them to me ' (Gal. iv. 15). But he sought not to please them with flattering words, only to save them. So faithful was he in this matter, and so conscious of his integrity, that he called God Himself into the witness-box. ' God is witness,' says he.

Blessed is the man who can call on God to witness for him; and that man in whom the Holy Spirit dwells in fullness can do this. Can you, my brother?

5. He was *not vain-glorious, nor dictatorial, nor oppressive.* Some men care nothing for money, but they care mightily for power and place and the glory that men give. But Paul was free from this spiritual itching. Listen to him: ' Nor of men sought we glory, neither of you, nor yet of others, when we might have been burdensome (or, used authority), as the apostles of Christ ' (1 Thess. ii. 6).

Said Solomon, ' For men to search their own glory is not glory ' (Prov. xxv. 27), it is only vain-glory. ' How can ye believe, which receive honour one of another, and seek not the honour that cometh from God only? ' asked Jesus (John v. 44).

From all this Paul was free, and so is every man who is full of the Holy Ghost. And it is only as we are thus free that with the whole heart and with a single eye we can devote ourselves to the work of saving men.

6. With all his boldness and faithfulness he was *gentle*. ' We were gentle among you,' he says, ' even as a nurse cherisheth her children ' (1 Thess. ii. 7).

The fierce hurricane which casts down the giant trees of the forest is not so mighty as the gentle sunshine, which, from tiny seeds and acorns, lifts aloft the towering spires of oak and fir on a thousand hills and mountains.

The wild storm that lashes the sea into foam and fury is feeble compared to the gentle, yet immeasurably powerful influence, which twice a day swings the oceans in resistless tides from shore to shore.

As in the physical world the mighty powers are gentle in their vast workings, so it is in the spiritual world. The light that falls on the lids of the sleeping infant and wakes it from its slumber, is not more gentle than the ' still small voice ' that brings assurance of forgiveness or cleansing to them that look unto Jesus.

Oh, the gentleness of God! ' Thy gentleness hath made me great,' said David (Ps. xviii. 35). ' I . . . beseech you by the meekness and gentleness of Christ ' (2 Cor. x. 1), wrote Paul. And again, ' The fruit of the Spirit is love, joy, peace, longsuffering, gentleness ' (Gal. v. 22). And as the Father, Son and Holy Ghost are gentle, so will be the servant of the Lord who is filled with the Spirit.

I shall never forget the gentleness of a mighty man of God whom I well knew, who on the platform was clothed with zeal as with a garment, and in his overwhelming earnestness was like a lion or a consuming fire; but when dealing with a wounded or broken heart, or with a seeking soul, no nurse with a little babe could be more tender than he.

7. Finally, Paul was full of *self-forgetful, self-sacrificing love.* ' So being affectionately desirous of you, we were willing to have imparted unto you, not the gospel of God only, but also our own souls, because ye were dear unto us ' (1 Thess. ii. 8).

No wonder he shook those heathen cities, overthrew their idols, had great revivals, his jailer was converted, and his converts would have gladly plucked out their eyes for him! Such tender, self-sacrificing love compels attention, begets confidence, enkindles love, and surely wins its object.

This burning love led him to labour and sacrifice, and so live and walk before them that he was not only a teacher, but an example of all he taught, and could safely say, ' Follow me.'

This love led him to preach the whole truth, that he might by all means save them. He kept back no truth because it was unpopular, for it was their salvation and not his own reputation and popularity he sought.

He preached not himself, but a crucified Christ, without the shedding of whose Blood there is no remission of sins; and through that precious Blood he preached present cleansing from all sin, and the gift of the Holy Spirit for all who obediently believe.

And this love kept him faithful and humble and true to the end, so that at last in sight of the martyr's death, he saw the martyr's crown and cried out: ' I am now ready to be offered . . . I have fought a good fight, I have finished my course, I have kept the faith: Henceforth there is laid up for me a crown of righteousness, which the Lord, the righteous judge, shall give me at that day ' (2 Tim. iv. 6-8).

He had been faithful, and now at the end he was oppressed with no doubts and harassed with no bitter regrets, but looked forward with eager joy to meeting his Lord and beholding the blessed face of Him whom he loved. Hallelujah!

Have you received the Holy Ghost?
'Twill fit you for the fight,
'Twill make of you a mighty host
To put your foes to flight.

Have you received the holy power?
'Twill fall from Heaven on you,
From Jesus' throne this very hour,
'Twill make you brave and true.

O now receive the holy fire!
'Twill burn away all dross,
All earthly, selfish, vain desire,
'Twill make you love the Cross.

' HAVE YE RECEIVED THE HOLY GHOST SINCE YE BELIEVED? '

CHAPTER XVII

Preaching

Ye shall receive power, after that the Holy Ghost is come upon you.'

'WHERE is the wise? where is the scribe? where
is the disputer of this world? hath not God made
foolish the wisdom of this world?' asks Paul.
And then he declares: 'After that in the wisdom of God
the world by wisdom knew not God, it pleased God by
the foolishness of preaching to save them that believe'
(1 Cor. i. 20, 21).

What kind of preaching is this? He does not say,
'foolish preaching', but the foolishness of such a way as
that of preaching. It is not the moral essay or the
intellectual, or semi-intellectual, kind of preaching that
is most generally heard throughout the world today,
that is to save men; for thousands of such sermons move
and convert no one. Nor is it a mere noisy declamation
called a sermon—noisy because empty of all earnest
thought and true feeling; but it must be the kind of
which Peter speaks when he writes of 'them that have
preached the gospel . . . with the Holy Ghost sent down
from Heaven' (1 Pet. i. 12).

No man is equipped to preach the gospel and undertake the spiritual oversight and instruction of souls, till
he has been anointed with the Holy Ghost.

The disciples had been led to Jesus by John the Baptist, whose mighty preaching laid a deep and broad
foundation for their spiritual education, and then for
three years they had listened to both the public and
private teachings of Jesus; they had been ' eye-witnesses
of His majesty ', of His life and death and resurrection,

and yet He commanded them to tarry in Jerusalem and wait for the Holy Spirit. He was to fit them for their ministry. And if they, trained and taught by the Master Himself, had need of the Holy Spirit to enable them to preach and testify with wisdom and power, how much more do you and I need His presence!

Without Him they could do nothing. With Him they were invincible and could continue the work of Jesus. The mighty energy of His working is seen in the preaching of Peter on the day of Pentecost. The sermon itself does not seem to have been very remarkable; indeed, it is principally composed of testimony backed up and fortified by Scripture quotations, followed by exhortation, just as are the sermons that are most effective today in the immediate conversion and sanctification of men. ' True preaching is a testimony,' said Horace Bushnell.

Peter's Scripture quotations were apt, fitting the occasion and the people to whom they were addressed. The testimony was bold and joyous, the rushing outflow of a warm, fresh throbbing experience; and the exhortation was burning, uncompromising in its demands, and yet tender and full of sympathy and love. But a divine Presence was at work in that vast, mocking, wondering throng, and it was He who made Peter's simple words search like fire, and carry such overwhelming conviction to the hearts of the people.

And it is still so that whenever and wherever a man preaches ' with the Holy Ghost sent down from Heaven ', there will be conviction.

Under Peter's sermon, ' they were pricked in their heart '. The truth pierced them as a sword until they said, ' What shall we do? ' They had been doubting and mocking a short time before, but now they were earnestly inquiring the way to be saved.

The speech may be without polish, the manner uncouth, and the matter simple and plain; but conviction will surely follow any preaching in the burning love and power and contagious joy of the Holy Spirit.

A few years ago a poor black boy in Africa, who had been stolen for a slave and most cruelly treated, heard a missionary talking of the indwelling of the Holy Spirit, and his heart hungered and thirsted for Him. In a strange manner he worked his way to New York to find out more about the Holy Spirit, getting the captain of the ship and several of the crew converted on the way. The brother in New York to whom he came took him to a meeting the first night he was in the city, and left him there while he went to fulfil another engagement. When he returned at a late hour, he found a crowd of men at the Penitent-form, led there by the simple words of this poor black fellow. He took him to his Sunday-school, and put him up to speak, while he attended to some other matters. When he turned from these affairs that had occupied his attention for only a little while, he found the Penitent-form full of teachers and scholars, weeping before the Lord. What the black boy had said he did not know; but he was bowed with wonder and filled with joy, for it was the power of the Holy Spirit.

Men used to fall as though cut down in battle under the preaching of Wesley, Whitefield, Finney and others. And while there may not be the same physical manifestation at all times, there will surely be the same opening of eyes to spiritual things, breaking of hearts and piercing of consciences. The Spirit under the preaching of a man filled with the Holy Ghost will often come upon a congregation like a wind, and heads will droop, eyes will brim with tears, and hearts will break under His convicting power. I remember a proud young woman who had been mercilessly criticizing us for several nights smitten in this way. She was smiling when suddenly the Holy Spirit winged a word to her heart, and instantly her countenance changed, her head drooped, and for an hour or more she sobbed and struggled while her proud heart broke; she found her way with true repentance and faith to the feet of Jesus, and her heavenly Father's favour. How often have we seen such sights as this under the preaching of the Founder! And it ought to be a common sight under the preaching of all servants of God; for what are we sent for but to convict men of their sin and their need, and by the power of the Spirit to lead them to the Saviour?

And not only will there be conviction under such preaching, but generally, if not always, there will be conversion and sanctification.

Three thousand people accepted Christ under Peter's pentecostal sermon. Later five thousand were converted, and a multitude of the priests were obedient to the faith. And it was so under the preaching of Philip in Samaria, of Peter in Lydda and Saron and in Cæsarea, and of Paul in Ephesus and other cities.

To be sure, the preaching of Stephen in its immediate effect only resulted in enraging his hearers until they stoned him to death; but it is highly probable that the ultimate result was the conversion of Paul, who kept the clothes of those who stoned him, and through Paul the evangelization of the Gentiles.

One of the greatest of American evangelists sought with agonizing prayers and tears the baptism with the Holy Spirit, and received it. He said he then preached the same sermons, but where before it had been as one beating the air, now hundreds were saved.

It is this that has made Salvation Army officers successful. Young, inexperienced, without special gifts and without learning, but with the baptism, they have been mighty to win souls. The hardest hearts have been broken, the darkest minds illuminated, the most stubborn wills subdued, and the wildest natures tamed. Their words have been with power and have convicted and converted and sanctified men, and whole communities have been transformed by their labours.

But without this Presence great gifts and profound and accurate learning are without avail in the salvation of men. We often see men with great natural powers, splendidly trained, and equipped with everything save this fiery baptism, who labour and preach year after year without seeing a soul saved. They have spent years in study; but they have not spent a day, much less ten days, fasting and praying and waiting upon God for His anointing that should fill them with heavenly wisdom and power for their work. They are like a great gun loaded and primed, but without a spark of fire to turn the powder and ball into a resistless lightning bolt.

Men need fire, and they get it from God in agonizing, wrestling, listening prayer that will not be denied; and when they get it, and not till then, will they preach with the Holy Ghost sent down from Heaven, and surely men shall be saved. Such preaching is not foolish.

1. It is *reasonable*. It takes account of man's reason and conforms to the dictates of common sense. We read that Paul reasoned with the people in the synagogues (Acts xvii. 2; xviii. 4, 19). His preaching was not a noisy harangue, nor a rose-water essay of pretty, empty platitudes, but a life and death—eternal life and death—grapple with the intelligence of men. God is the Author of man's intellectual powers, and He endowed him with reason. The Holy Spirit respects these powers, and appeals to reason when He inspires a man to preach to his fellows.

2. It is *persuasive*. ' Come now, and let us reason together, saith the Lord ' (Isa. 1. 18). He takes account of man's feelings, sensibilities, fears, hopes and affections, and persuades them. It appeals to the whole man. Man is not all intellect, a mere logic machine. He is a bundle of sensibilities as well; and true preaching —the kind that is inspired by the Holy Ghost—appeals to the intelligence of men with reasons and arguments. But they are penetrated through and through with such a spirit of compassionate persuasiveness, that wholesome fears are aroused, shame of sin is created, conscience is unshackled, desires for purity and goodness are resurrected, tender affections are quickened, the will is energized, and the whole man is fired and illuminated by

a flame of saving emotions, kindled by the fire in the preacher's heart, that enables him to see and feel the realities of things eternal, of God and Judgment, and of Heaven and Hell, of the final fixedness of moral character, of the importance of immediate repentance, and acceptance of God's offer of mercy in Jesus Christ.

3. It is *scriptural*. The gospel is not opposed to natural religion and reason, but it has run far ahead of them. It is a revelation from God of facts, of grace and truth, of mercy and love and of a plan of redemption that man could not discover for himself. And this revelation is recorded in the Scriptures. So we find that Paul ' reasoned with them out of the Scriptures '. The truths of the Bible cover man's moral needs as a glove covers his hand; fits his moral nature and experience as a key fits its lock; reveals the condition of his heart as a mirror reveals the state of his face.

No man can read the Bible thoughtfully without either hating it or hating his sins.

But, while it reveals man's sin and his lost condition, it at the same time declares God's love and His plan of redemption. It shows us Jesus Christ and the way by which we come to Him, and through Him get deliverance from sin and become a new creation. It is in the Bible, and only there, that this revelation can be found. And it is this the Holy Ghost inspires men to preach.

' We preach Christ crucified,' wrote Paul (1 Cor. i. 23); and again, ' We preach not ourselves, but Christ Jesus the Lord ' (2 Cor. iv. 5). And he exhorted Timothy to ' preach the word ' (2 Tim. iv. 2). It is ' the unsearchable ', but revealed, ' riches of Christ ' that we are to preach (Eph. iii. 8).

The Holy Spirit makes the word alive. He brings it to the remembrance of the preachers in whom He abides, and He applies it to the heart of the hearers, lightening up the soul as with a sun until sin is seen in all its hideousness, or cutting as a sharp sword, piercing the heart with resistless conviction of the guilt and shame of sin.

Peter had no time to consult the Scriptures and prepare a sermon on the morning of Pentecost; but the Holy Spirit quickened his memory, and brought to his mind the Scriptures appropriate to the occasion.

Hundreds of years before, the Holy Spirit, by the mouth of the prophet Joel, had foretold that in the last days the Spirit should be poured out upon all flesh, and that their sons and daughters should prophesy (ii. 28-32). And the same Spirit that spoke through Joel now made Peter to see and declare that this pentecostal baptism was that of which Joel spoke.

By the mouth of David He had said: ' Thou wilt not leave my soul in hell; neither wilt Thou suffer Thine Holy One to see corruption ' (Ps. xvi. 10); and now Peter, by the inspiration of the same Spirit, applies this Scripture to the resurrection of Jesus, and so proves to the Jews that the One they had condemned and killed was the Holy One foretold in prophecy and psalm.

And so today the Holy Spirit inspires men who receive Him to use the Scriptures to awaken, convict and save men.

When Finney was a young preacher, he was invited to a country school-house to preach. On the way there he became much distressed in soul, and his mind seemed blank and dark, when all at once the words spoken to Lot in Sodom by the angels came to his mind: ' Up, get you out of this place; for the Lord will destroy this city ' (Gen. xix. 14). He explained the text, told the people about Lot and the wickedness of Sodom, and applied it to them. While he spoke they began to look exceedingly angry, and then, as he earnestly exhorted them to give up their sins and seek the Lord, they began to fall from their seats as though stricken down in battle, and to cry to God for mercy. A great revival followed; many were converted, and a number of the converts became ministers of the gospel.

To Finney's amazement, he learned afterward that the place was called Sodom because of its extreme wicked-

ness, and the old man who had invited him to preach
was called Lot, because he was the only God-fearing
man in the place. Evidently the Holy Spirit worked
through Finney to accomplish these results. And such
inspiration is not uncommon with those who are filled
with the Spirit.

But this reinforcement of the mind and memory by
the Holy Spirit does not do away with the need of study.
The Spirit quickens that which is already in the mind
and memory, as the warm sun and rains of spring
quicken the sleeping seeds that are in the ground, and
only those. The sun does not put the seed in the soil,
nor does the Holy Spirit without our attention and study
put the word of God in our minds. For that we should
prayerfully and patiently study.

' We will give ourselves continually to prayer, and to
the ministry of the word,' said the apostles (Acts vi. 4).

' Study to shew thyself approved unto God, a workman
that needeth not to be ashamed, rightly dividing the
word of truth,' wrote Paul to Timothy (2 Tim. ii. 15).

Those men have been best able to divide rightly the
word, and have been most mightily used by the Holy
Spirit, who have most carefully and prayerfully studied
the word of God, and most constantly and lovingly
meditated upon it.

4. This preaching is *healing and comforting*. Preaching
' with the Holy Ghost sent down from Heaven ' is
indescribably searching in its effects. But it is also
edifying, strengthening, comforting to those who are
wholly the Lord's. It cuts, but only to cure. It searches,
but only to save. It is constructive, as well as destructive.
It tears down sin and pride and unbelief, but it builds up
faith and righteousness and holiness and all the graces of
a Christian character. It warms the heart with love,
strengthens faith, and confirms the will in all holy
purposes.

Every preacher baptized with the Holy Ghost can
say with Jesus: ' The Spirit of the Lord is upon Me

because He hath anointed Me to preach the gospel to the poor; He hath sent Me to heal the brokenhearted, to preach deliverance to the captives, and recovering of sight to the blind, to set at liberty them that are bruised, To preach the acceptable year of the Lord ' (Luke iv. 18, 19).

Seldom is there a congregation in which there are only those who need to be convicted. There will also be meek and gentle ones to whom should be brought a message of joy and good tidings; broken-hearted ones to be bound up; wounded ones to heal; tempted ones to be delivered; and those whom Satan has bound by some fear or habit to be set free; and the Holy Spirit who knows all hearts will inspire the word that shall bless these needy ones.

The preacher filled with the Holy Spirit, who is instant in prayer, constant in the study of God's word, and steadfast and active in faith, will surely be so helped that he can say: ' The Lord God hath given me the tongue of the learned, that I should know how to speak a word in season to him that is weary ' (Isa. l. 4). And as with little Samuel, the Lord will ' let none of his words fall to the ground ' (1 Sam. iii. 19).

He will expect results, and God will make them follow his preaching as surely as corn follows the planting and cultivating of the farmer.

' HAVE YE RECEIVED THE HOLY GHOST SINCE YE BELIEVED? '

CHAPTER XVIII

The Holy Spirit's Call to the Work

' Ye shall receive power, after that the Holy Ghost is come upon you.'

'THE Spirit of the Lord God is upon Me; because the Lord hath anointed Me to preach good tidings unto the meek; He hath sent Me ' (Isa. lxi. 1), is the testimony of the workman God sends.

God chooses His own workmen, and it is the office of the Holy Spirit to call whom He will to preach the gospel. I doubt not He calls men to other employments for His glory, and would still more often do so, if men would but listen and wait upon Him to know His will.

He called Bezaleel and Aholiab to build the tabernacle. He called and commissioned the Gentile king, Cyrus, to rebuild Jerusalem and restore His chastised and humbled people to their own land. And did He not call Joan of Arc to her strange and wonderful mission? And Washington and Lincoln?

And, no doubt, He *leads* most men by His providence to their life-work; but the call to preach the gospel is more than a providential leading; it is a distinct and imperative conviction.

Bishop Simpson, in his *Lectures on Preaching*, says:

> Even in its faintest form there is this distinction between a call to the ministry and a choice of other professions: a young man may *wish* to be a physician; he may *desire* to enter the navy; he would *like* to be a farmer; but he feels he *ought* to be a minister. It is this feeling of *ought*, or obligation, which in its feeblest form indicates the divine call. It is not in the aptitude, taste or desire, but in the conscience, that its root is found. It is the voice of God to the human conscience, saying, ' You ought to preach.'

Sometimes the call comes as distinctly as though a

voice had spoken from the skies into the depths of the heart.

A young man who was studying law was converted. After a while he was convicted for sanctification, and while seeking he heard, as it were, a voice, saying, ' Will you devote all your time to the Lord? ' He replied: ' I am to be a lawyer, not a preacher, Lord.' But not until he had said, ' Yes, Lord ', could he find the blessing.

A thoughtless, godless young fellow was working in the corn-field when a telegram was handed him announcing the death of his brother, a brilliant and devoted Salvation Army field officer; and there and then, unsaved as he was, God called him, showed him a vast Army with ranks broken, where his brother had fallen, and made him to feel that he should fill the breach in the ranks. Fourteen months later he took up the sword and entered the Fight from the same platform on which his brother fell, and is today one of our most successful and promising field officers.

Again, the call may come as a quiet suggestion, a gentle conviction, as though a gossamer bridle were placed upon the heart and conscience to guide the man into the work of the Lord. The suggestion gradually becomes clearer, the conviction strengthens until it masters the man, and if he seeks to escape it, he finds the silken bridle to be one of stoutest thongs and firmest steel.

It was so with me. When but a boy of eleven I heard a man preaching, and I said to myself, ' Oh, how beautiful to preach! ' Two years later I was converted, and soon the conviction came upon me that I should preach. Later, I decided to follow another profession; but the conviction increased in strength, while I struggled against it, and turned away my ears and went on with my studies. Yet in every crisis or hour of stillness, when my soul faced God, the conviction that I must preach burned itself deeper into my conscience. I rebelled against it. I felt I would almost rather (but not quite) go to Hell than to submit. Then at last a great 'woe is unto me, if I preach not the gospel ', took possession of me, and I yielded, and God won. Hallelujah!

The first year He gave me three revivals, with many souls; and now I would rather preach Jesus to poor sinners and feed His lambs than to be an archangel before the Throne. Some day, some day, He will call me into His blessed presence, and I shall stand before His face, and praise Him for ever for counting me worthy and calling me to preach His glad gospel and share in His joy of saving the lost. The ' woe ' is lost in love and delight through the baptism of the Spirit and the sweet assurance that Jesus is pleased.

Occasionally, the call comes to a man who is ready and responds promptly and gladly. When Isaiah received the fiery touch that purged his life and purified his heart, he ' heard the voice of the Lord, saying, Whom shall I send, and who will go for us? ' And in the joy and power of his new experience, he cried out, ' Here am I; send me ' (Isa. vi. 8).

When Paul received his call, he says, ' Immediately I conferred not with flesh and blood ' (Gal. i. 16), and he got up and went as the Lord led him.

But more often it seems the Lord finds men pre-occupied with other plans and ambitions, or encompassed with obstacles and difficulties, or oppressed with a deep sense of unworthiness or unfitness. Moses argued that he could not talk: ' O my Lord, I am not eloquent, neither heretofore, nor since Thou hast spoken unto Thy servant: but I am slow of speech, and of a slow tongue.'

And then the Lord condescended, as He always does, to reason with the backward man. ' Who hath made man's mouth? or who maketh the dumb, or deaf, or the seeing, or the blind? have not I the Lord? Now therefore go, and I will be with thy mouth, and teach thee what thou shalt say ' (Exod. iv. 10-12).

When the call of God came to Jeremiah, he shrank back, and said, ' Ah, Lord God! behold, I cannot speak:

for I am a child.' But the Lord replied: ' Say not, I am a child: for thou shalt go to all that I shall send thee, and whatsoever I command thee thou shalt speak. Be not afraid of their faces: for I am with thee to deliver thee ' (Jer. i. 6-8).

And so the call of God comes today to those who shrink and feel that they are the most unfit, or most hedged in by insuperable difficulties.

I know a man, who, when converted, could not tell A from B. He knew nothing whatever about the Bible, and stammered so badly that, when asked his own name, it would usually take him a minute or so to tell it; added to this, he lisped badly, and was subject to a nervous affliction which seemed likely to unfit him for any kind of work whatever. But God poured light and love into his heart, called him to preach, and today he is one of the mightiest soul-winners in the whole round of my acquaintance. When he speaks the house is always packed to the doors, and the people hang on his words with wonder and joy.

He was converted at a camp meeting, and sanctified wholly in a corn field. He learned to read; but, being too poor to afford a light in the evening, he studied a large-print Bible by the light of the full moon. Today, he has the Bible almost committed to memory, and when he speaks he does not open the book, but reads his lesson from memory and quotes proof texts from Genesis to Revelation without mistake, giving chapter and verse for every quotation. When he talks his face shines, and his speech is like honey for sweetness and like bullets fired from a gun for power. He is one of the weak and foolish ones God has chosen to confound the wise and mighty (1 Cor. i. 27).

If God calls a man, He will so corroborate the call in some way that men may know that there is a prophet among them. It will be with him as it was with Samuel. ' And Samuel grew, and the Lord was with him, and did let none of His words fall to the ground. And all Israel from Dan even to Beer-sheba knew that Samuel was established to be a prophet of the Lord ' (1 Sam. iii. 19, 20).

If the man himself is uncertain about the call, God will deal patiently with him to make him certain, as He did with Gideon. His fleece will be wet with dew when the earth is dry, or dry when the earth is wet; or he will hear of some tumbling barley cake smiting the tents of Midian, that will strengthen his faith and make him to know that God is with him (Judges vi. 36-40; vii. 9-15).

If the door is shut and difficulties hedge the way, God will go before the man He calls and open the door and sweep away the difficulties (Isa. xlv. 2, 3).

If others think the man so ignorant and unfit that they doubt his call, God will give him such grace or such power to win souls that they shall have to acknowledge that God has chosen him. It was in this way that God made a whole National Headquarters, from the Commissioner downward, to know that He had chosen the elevator boy for His work. The boy got scores of his passengers on the elevator saved, and then he was commissioned and sent into the Field to devote all his time to saving men.

The Lord will surely let man's comrades and brethren know, as surely as He did the church at Antioch, when ' the Holy Ghost said, Separate Me Barnabas and Saul for the work whereunto I have called them ' (Acts xiii. 2).

Sometimes the one who is called will try to hide it in his heart, and then God stirs up some officer or minister, some soldier or mother in Israel, to lay a hand on his shoulders, and ask, ' Are you not called to the work? ' and he finds he cannot hide himself or escape from the call, any more than could Adam hide himself from God behind the trees of the garden, or Jonah escape God's call by taking ship for Tarshish.

Happy is the man who does not try to escape, but, though trembling at the mighty responsibility, assumes it and, with all humility and faithfulness, sets to work by prayer and patient, continuous study of God's word to fit himself for God's work. He will need to prepare himself, for the call to the work is also a call to preparation, continuous preparation of the fullest possible kind.

The man whom God calls cannot safely neglect or despise the call. He will find his mission on earth, his happiness and peace, his power and prosperity, his reward in Heaven, and probably Heaven itself, bound up with that call and dependent upon it. He may run away from it, as did Jonah, and find a waiting ship to favour his flight; but he will also find fierce storms and billowing seas overtaking him, and big-mouthed fishes of trouble and disaster ready to swallow him.

But if he heeds the call and cheerfully goes where God appoints, God will go with him; he shall nevermore be left alone. The Holy Spirit will surely accompany him, and he may be one of the happiest men on earth, one of the gladdest creatures in God's universe.

' Lo, I am with you alway, even unto the end of the world,' said Jesus, as He commissioned His disciples to go to all nations and preach the gospel (Matt. xxviii. 20). ' My presence shall go with thee,' said Jehovah to Moses (Exod. xxxiii. 14).

And to the boy Jeremiah, He said, ' Be not afraid of their faces: for I am with thee to deliver thee. . . . And they shall fight against thee; but they shall not prevail against thee; for I am with thee ' (Jer. i. 8, 19).

I used to read these words with a great and rapturous joy, as I realized by faith that they were also meant for me and for every man sent of God, and that His blessed presence was with me every time I spoke to the people or dealt with an individual soul or knelt in prayer with a penitent seeker after God; and I still read them so.

Has He called you into the work, my brother? And are you conscious of His helpful, sympathizing, loving presence with you? If so, let no petty offence, hardship, danger, or dread of the future cause you to turn aside or draw back. Stick to the work till He calls you out, and when He so calls you can go with open face and a heart abounding with love, joy and peace, and He will still go with you.

' HAVE YE RECEIVED THE HOLY GHOST SINCE YE BELIEVED ? '

CHAPTER XIX

The Sheathed Sword : A Law of the Spirit

' Ye shall receive power, after that the Holy Ghost is come upon you.'

JUST as the moss and the oak are higher in the order of creation than the clod of clay and the rock, the bird and beast than the moss and the oak, the man than the bird and the beast, so the spiritual man is a higher being than the natural man. The sons of God are a new order of being. The Christian is a ' new creation '. Just as there are laws governing the life of the plant, and other and higher laws that of the bird and beast, so there are higher laws for man, and still higher for the Christian. It was with regard to one of these higher laws that govern the heavenly life of the Christian that Jesus said to Peter, ' Put up thy sword.'

Jesus said to Pilate, ' My kingdom is not of this world: if My kingdom were of this world, then would My servants fight ' (John xviii. 36). The natural man is a fighter. It is the law of his carnal nature. He fights with fist and sword, tongue and wit. His kingdom is of this world and he fights for it with such weapons as this world furnishes. The Christian is a citizen of Heaven and is subject to its law, which is universal, whole-hearted love. In his Kingdom he conquers not by fighting, but by submitting. When an enemy takes his coat, he overcomes him, not by going to law, but by generously giving him his cloak also. When his enemy compels him to go a mile with him, he vanquishes the enemy by cheerfully going two miles with him. When he is smitten on one cheek, he wins his foe by meekly turning the other cheek. This is the law of the new life from Heaven, and only by recognizing and obeying it can that new life be

sustained and passed on to others. This is the narrow
way which leads to life eternal, ' and few there be that
find it ' or, finding it, are willing to walk in it.

A Russian peasant, Sutajeff, could get no help from
the religious teachers of his village, so he learned to read;
and while studying the Bible he found this narrow way
and walked gladly in it. One night neighbours stole
some of his grain, but in their haste or carelessness they
left a bag. He found it, and ran after them to restore it
' for ', said he, ' fellows who have to steal must be hard
up.' And by this Christlike spirit he saved both himself
and them, for he kept the spirit of love in his own heart
and they were converted and became his most ardent
disciples.

A beggar woman to whom he gave lodging stole the
bedding and ran away with it. She was pursued by the
neighbours, and was just about to be put in prison when
Sutajeff appeared, became her advocate, secured her
acquittal, and gave her food and money for her
journey.

He recognized the law of his new life and gladly
obeyed it, and so was not overcome of evil, but persistently and triumphantly overcame evil with good (Rom.
xii. 21).

This is the spirit and method of Jesus; and by men
filled with this spirit and following this method He will
yet win the world.

He came ' not to be ministered unto, but to minister,
and to give His life a ransom for many ' (Mark x. 45).
His spirit is not one of self-seeking, but of self-sacrifice.
Some mysterious majesty of His presence or voice so
awed and overcame His foes that they went back and
fell to the ground before Him in the Garden of His
agony, but He meekly submitted Himself to them; and
when Peter laid to with his sword and cut off the ear
of the high priest's servant, Jesus said to him, ' Put up
thy sword into the sheath: the cup which My Father
hath given Me, shall I not drink it? ' (John xviii. 11).

This was the spirit of Isaac. When he digged a well the Philistines strove with his servants for it; so he digged another; and when they strove for that, he removed and digged yet another, ' and for that they strove not: and he called the name of it Rehoboth (room); and he said, For now the Lord hath made room for us, and we shall be fruitful in the land. . . . And the Lord appeared unto him the same night, and said, I am the God of Abraham thy father: fear not, for I am with thee, and will bless thee, and multiply thy seed ' (Gen. xxvi. 22, 24).

This was the spirit of David when Saul was hunting for his life; twice David could have slain him, and when urged to do so, he said, ' As the Lord liveth, the Lord shall smite him; or his day shall come to die; or he shall descend into battle and perish. The Lord forbid that I should stretch forth mine hand against the Lord's anointed ' (1 Sam. xxvi. 10, 11).

This was the spirit of Paul. He says, ' Being reviled, we bless; being persecuted, we suffer it: Being defamed, we intreat ' (1 Cor. iv. 12, 13). ' The servant of the Lord must not strive; but be gentle unto all men ' (2 Tim. ii. 24). This is the spirit of our King, this is the law of His kingdom.

Is this your spirit? When you are reviled, bemeaned and slandered, and are tempted to retort, He says to you, ' Put up thy sword into the sheath.' When you are wronged and ill-treated, and men ride rough-shod over you, and you feel it but just to smite back, He says, ' Put up thy sword into the sheath.' ' Live peaceably with all men ' (Rom. xii. 18). Your weapons are not carnal, but spiritual, now that you belong to Him and have your citizenship in Heaven. If you fight with the sword; if you retort and smite back when you are wronged, you quench the Spirit; you get out of the narrow way, and your new life from Heaven will perish.

An officer went to a hard corps, and after a while

found that his predecessor was sending back to friends for money which his own corps much needed. He felt it to be an injustice and, losing sight of the spirit of Jesus, he made a complaint about it, and the money was returned. But he got lean in his soul. He had quenched the Spirit. He had broken the law of the Kingdom. He had not only refused to give his cloak, but had fought for and secured the return of the coat. He had lost the smile of Jesus, and his poor heart was sad and heavy within him. He came to me with anxious inquiry as to what I thought of his action. I had to admit that the other man had transgressed and that the money ought to be returned, but that he should have been more grieved over the unchristlike spirit of his brother than over the loss of the five dollars, and that like Sutajeff he should have said, ' Poor fellow! He must be hard up; I will send him five dollars myself. He has taken my coat, he shall have my cloak too.' When I told him that story, he came to himself very quickly and was soon back in the narrow way and rejoicing in the smile of Jesus once again.

' But will not people walk over us, if we do not stand up for our rights?' you ask. I do not argue that you are not to stand up for your rights; but that you are to stand up for your higher rather than your lower rights, the rights of your heavenly life rather than your earthly life, and that you are to stand up for your rights in the way and spirit of Jesus rather than in the way and spirit of the world.

If men wrong you intentionally, they wrong themselves far worse than they wrong you; and if you have the spirit of Jesus in your heart you will pity them more than you pity yourself. They nailed Jesus to the Cross and hung Him up to die; they gave Him gall and vinegar to drink; they cast votes for His seamless robe, and divided His garments between them, while the crowd wagged their heads at Him and mocked Him. Great was the injustice and wrong they were inflicting upon Him, but He was not filled with anger, only pity. He thought not of the wrong done Him, but of the wrong they did themselves, and their sin against His heavenly Father, and He prayed not for judgment upon them, but that they might be forgiven, and He won them, and is winning and will win the world.   Bless God!

' By mercy and truth iniquity is purged,' wrote Solomon (Prov. xvi. 6).   ' Put up thy sword into the sheath ', and take mercy and truth for your weapons, and God will be with you and for you, and great shall be your victory and joy.   Hallelujah!

' HAVE YE RECEIVED THE HOLY GHOST SINCE YE BELIEVED ? '

CHAPTER XX

Victory through the Holy Spirit over Suffering

' Ye shall receive power, after that the Holy Ghost is come upon you.'

HAD there been no sin our heavenly Father would have found other means by which to develop in us passive virtues, and train us in the graces of meekness, patience, long-suffering and forbearance, which so beautify and display the Christian character. But since sin is here, with its contradictions and falsehoods, its darkness, its wars, brutalities and injustices, producing awful harvests of pain and sorrow, God, in wonderful wisdom and lovingkindness, turns even these into instruments by which to fashion in us beautiful graces. Storm succeeds sunshine, and darkness the light; pain follows hard on the heels of pleasure, while sorrow peers over the shoulder of joy; gladness and grief, rest and toil, peace and war, interminably intermingled, follow each other in ceaseless succession in this world. We cannot escape suffering while in the body. But we can receive it with a faith that robs it of its terror and extracts from it richest blessing; from the flinty rock will gush forth living waters, and the carcase of the lion will furnish the sweetest honey.

This is so even when the suffering is a result of our own folly or sin. It is intended not only in some measure as a punishment, but also as a teacher, a corrective, a remedy, a warning; and it will surely work for good if, instead of repining and vainly regretting the past, we steadily look unto Jesus and learn our lesson in patience and thankfulness.

If all the skies were sunshine,
　　Our faces would be fain
To feel once more upon them
　　The cooling plash of rain.

If all the world were music,
　　Our hearts would often long
For one sweet strain of silence
　　To break the endless song.

If life were always merry,
　　Our souls would seek relief
And rest from weary laughter
　　In the quiet arms of grief.

Doubtless all our suffering is a result of sin, but not necessarily the sin of the sufferer. Jesus was the sinless One, but He was also the chief of sufferers. Paul's great and lifelong sufferings came upon him, not because of his sins, but rather because he had forsaken sin, and was following Jesus in a world of sin and seeking the salvation of his fellows. In this path there is no escape from suffering, though there are hidden and unspeakable consolations. ' In the world ye shall have tribulation,' said Jesus (John xvi. 33). ' All that will live godly in Christ Jesus shall suffer persecution,' wrote Paul (2 Tim. iii. 12).

Sooner or later, suffering in some form comes to each of us. It may come through broken health, or pain and weariness of body; or through mental anguish, moral distress, spiritual darkness and uncertainty. It may come through the loss of loved ones, through betrayal by trusted friends; or through deferred or ruined hopes, or base ingratitude; or perhaps in unrequited toil and sacrifice and ambitions all unfulfilled. Nothing more clearly distinguishes the man filled with the Spirit from the man who is not than the way each receives suffering.

One with triumphant faith and shining face and strong heart glories in tribulation, and counts it all joy. To this class belong the apostles, who, beaten and threatened, ' departed from the presence of the council, rejoicing that they were counted worthy to suffer shame for His name ' (Acts v. 41).

The other with doubts and fears, murmurs and complains, adds to his other miseries that of a rebellious heart and discontented mind.   One sees the enemy's armed host, and unmixed distress and danger; the other sees the angel of the Lord, with abundant succour and safety (Ps. xxxiv. 7).

An evangelist of my acquaintance told a story that illustrates this.   When a pastor, he went one morning to visit two sisters who were greatly afflicted.   They were about the same age, and had long been professing Christians and members of the church.   He asked the first one upon whom he called, ' How is it with you this morning? '   ' Oh, I have not slept all night,' she replied. ' I have so much pain.   It is so hard to have to lie here. I cannot see why God deals so with me.'   Evidently she was not filled with the Spirit, but was in a controversy with the Lord about her sufferings and would not be comforted.

Leaving her he called immediately upon the other sister, and asked, ' How are you today? '   ' Oh, I had such a night of suffering! ' she replied.   Then there came out upon her worn face a beautiful radiance, and she added, ' But Jesus was so near and helped me so, that I could suffer this way and more, if my Father thinks best.'   On she went with like words of cheer and triumph that made the sick room a vestibule of glory. No lack of comfort in her heart, for the Comforter Himself, the Holy Spirit, had been invited and had come in. One had the Comforter in fullness, the other had not.

Probably no man ever suffered more than Paul, but with soldier-like fortitude he bore his heavy burdens, faced his constant and exacting labours, endured his sore trials, disappointments and bitter persecutions by fierce and relentless enemies; he stood unmoved amid shipwrecks, stripes and imprisonments, cold, hunger and homelessness without a whimper that might suggest

repining or discouragement, or an appeal for pity.
Indeed, he went beyond simple uncomplaining fortitude
and said, ' we glory in tribulations ' (Rom. v. 3); ' I
am exceeding joyful in all our tribulation ' (2 Cor. vii. 4);
' I take pleasure in infirmities, in reproaches, in necessities, in persecutions, in distresses for Christ's sake '
(2 Cor. xii. 10).   After a terrible scourging upon his
bare back, he was thrust into a loathsome inner dungeon,
his feet fast in the stocks, with worse things probably
awaiting him on the morrow.   Nevertheless, we find
him and Silas, his companion in suffering, at midnight
praying and singing praises unto God (Acts xvi. 25).

What is his secret?   Listen to him: ' Because the love
of God is shed abroad in our hearts by the Holy Ghost
which is given unto us ' (Rom. v. 5).   His prayer for
his Ephesian brethren had been answered in his own
heart: 'That He would grant you, according to the
riches of His glory, to be strengthened with might by His
Spirit in the inner man; That Christ may dwell in your
hearts by faith ' (Eph. iii. 16, 17).   And this inner
strength and consciousness, through faith in an indwelling Christ, enabled him to receive suffering and trial,
not stoically as the Red Indian, nor hilariously, in a
spirit of bravado, but cheerfully and with a thankful
heart.

Arnold of Rugby has written something about his
' most dear and blessed sister ' that illustrates the power
flowing from exhaustless fountains of inner joy and
strength through the working of the Holy Spirit.   He
says:

> I never saw a more perfect instance of the spirit and power
> of love and of a sound mind.   Her life was a daily martyrdom
> for twenty years, during which she adhered to her early-
> formed resolution of never talking about herself; she was
> thoughtful about the very pins and ribands of my wife's dress,
> about the making of a doll's cap for a child—but of herself,
> save only as regarded her ripening in all goodness, wholly
> thoughtless, enjoying everything lovely, graceful, beautiful,
> high-minded, whether in God's works or man's, with the
> keenest relish; inheriting the earth to the very fullness of the

promise, though never leaving her crib, nor changing her posture; and preserved, through the very valley of the shadow of death, from all fear or impatience, and from every cloud of impaired reason, which might mar the beauty of Christ's and the Spirit's work.

It is not by hypnotizing the soul, nor by blessing it into a state of ecstatic insensibility, that the Lord enables the man filled with the Spirit thus to triumph over suffering. Rather it is by giving the soul a sweet, constant and unshaken assurance through faith. First, that it is freely and fully accepted in Christ. Second, that whatever suffering comes, it is measured, weighed, permitted by love infinitely tender and guided by wisdom that cannot err. Third, that however difficult it may be to explain suffering now, it is nevertheless *one* of the ' all things ' which ' work together for good to them that love God ' (Rom. viii. 28), and that in a ' little while ' it will not only be swallowed up in the ineffable blessedness and glory, but that in some way it is actually helping to work out ' a far more exceeding and eternal weight of glory ' (2 Cor. iv. 17). Fourth, that though the furnace has been heated seven times hotter than was wont, yet there is walking with us in the fire One whose ' form . . . is like the Son of God ' (Dan. iii. 25); though triumphant enemies have thrust us into the lions' den, yet the angel of the Lord arrived first and locked the lions' jaws; though foes may have formed against us sharp weapons, yet they cannot prosper, for His shield and buckler defend us; though all things be lost, yet ' Thou remainest '; and though ' my flesh and my heart faileth . . . God is the strength of my heart, and my portion for ever ' (Ps. lxxiii. 26).

Not all God's dear children thus triumph over their difficulties and sufferings, but this is God's standard, and they may attain unto it if, by faith, they will open their hearts and ' be filled with the Spirit '.

Here is the testimony of a Salvation Army officer:

Viewed from the outside, my life as a sinner was easy and untroubled, over which most of my friends expressed envy;

while these same friends thought my life as a Christian full of care, toil, hardship and immense loss. This, however, was only an outside view, and the real state of the case was exactly the opposite of what they supposed. For in all the pleasure-seeking, idleness, and freedom from responsibility of my life apart from God, I carried an immeasurable burden of fear, anxiety and constantly recurring disappointment; trifles weighed upon me, and the thought of death haunted me with vague terrors.

But when I gave myself wholly to God, though my lot became at once one of toil, responsibility, comparative poverty and sacrifice, yet I could not feel pain in any storm that broke over my head, because of the presence of God. It was not so much that I was insensible to trouble, as sensible of His presence and love; and the worst trials were as nothing in my sight, nor have been for over twenty-two years. While as for death, it appears only as a doorway into more abundant life, and I can alter an old German hymn and sing with joy:

> O how my heart with rapture dances
> To think my dying hour advances!
> Then, Lord, with Thee!
> My Lord, with Thee!

This is faith's triumph over the worst the world can offer through the blessed fullness of the indwelling Comforter. Bless His name!

> Joy of the desolate, light of the straying,
>   Hope of the penitent, Advocate sure;
> Here speaks the Comforter, tenderly saying,
>   Earth has no sorrow that Heaven cannot cure.

'HAVE YE RECEIVED THE HOLY GHOST SINCE YE BELIEVED?'

CHAPTER XXI

The Overflowing Blessing

' Ye shall receive power, after that the Holy Ghost is come upon you.'

THE children of Israel were instructed by Moses to give tithes of all they had to the Lord, and in return God promised richly to bless them, making their fields and vineyards fruitful and causing their flocks and herds safely to multiply. But they became covetous and unbelieving, and began to rob God by withholding their tithes, and then God began to withhold His blessing from them.

But still God loved and pitied them, and sent to them again and again by His prophets. Finally He said: ' Bring ye all the tithes into the storehouse, that there may be meat in Mine house, and prove Me now herewith, saith the Lord of hosts, if I will not open you the windows of heaven, and pour you out a blessing, that there shall not be room enough to receive it ' (Mal. iii. 10).

He promised to make their barns overflow, if they would be faithful, if they would pay their tithes and discharge their obligations to Him.

Now, this overflow of barns and granaries is a type of overflowing hearts and lives when we give ourselves fully to God, and the blessed Holy Ghost comes in and Jesus becomes all and in all to us. The blessing is too big to contain, but just bursts out and overflows through the life, the looks, the conversation, the very tones of the voice, and gladdens and refreshes and purifies wherever it goes. Jesus calls it ' rivers of living water ' (John vii. 38).

There is an overflow of *love*. Sin brings in an overflow of hate, so that the world is filled with wars and murders, slanders, oppression and selfishness. But this blessing causes love to overflow. Schools, colleges and hospitals are built; shelters, rescue homes and orphanages are opened; even war itself is in some measure humanized by the Red Cross Society and Christian commissions. Sinners love their own, but this blessing makes us to love all men—strangers, the heathen, and even our enemies.

There is an overflow of *peace*. It settles old quarrels and grudges. It makes a different atmosphere in the home. The children know it when father and mother get the Comforter. Kindly words and sweet goodwill take the place of bitterness and strife. I suspect that even the dumb beasts realize the overflow.

I heard a laughable story of a man whose cow would switch her tail in his face, and then kick over the pail when he was milking her. Then he would give her a beating with the stool on which he sat. But he got the blessing, and his heart was overflowing with peace. The next morning he went to milk that cow, and when the pail was nearly full, swish! came the tail in his face; with a vicious kick she knocked over the pail, and then ran across the barn-yard. The blessed man picked up the empty pail and stool and went over to the cow, which stood trembling, awaiting the usual kicks and beating; but instead he patted her gently and said, ' You may kick over that pail as often as you please, but I am not going to beat you any more.' The cow seemed to understand, for she dropped her head and quietly began to eat. She never kicked again! That story is good enough to be true, and I doubt not it is, for certainly when the Comforter comes a great peace fills the heart and overflows through all the life.

There is an overflow of *joy*. It makes the face to shine; it glances from the eye and bubbles out in thanksgiving and praise. You never can tell when one who has the

blessing will shout out, ' Glory to God! Praise the
Lord! Hallelujah! Amen!'

I have sometimes seen a whole congregation wakened
up and refreshed and made glad by the joyous overflow
from one clean-hearted soul. A salvation soldier or
officer with an overflow of genuine joy is worth a whole
company of ordinary folk. He is a host within himself,
and is a living proof of the text, ' The joy of the Lord is
your strength ' (Neh. viii. 10).

There is an overflow of *patience* and *long-suffering*.
When a man got this blessing, his wicked wife was so
enraged that she left him and went across the way and
lived as the wife of his unmarried brother. He was
terribly tempted to take his gun and go over and kill
them both. But he prayed about it, and the Lord gave
him the patience and long-suffering of Jesus, who bears
long with the backslider who leaves Him and joins
himself with the world. The man continued to treat
them with the utmost kindness, as though they had done
him no wrong. Some people might say he was weak,
but I should say he was unusually ' strong in the grace
of our Lord Jesus Christ ', and one of his neighbours
told me that they all believed in his religion.

There is an overflow of *goodness* and *generosity*. I read
the other day of a poor man who supports eight workers
in the foreign mission field. When asked how he did it,
he replied that he wore celluloid collars, did his own
washing, denied himself and managed his affairs in order
to do it.

Do you ask, ' How can I get such a blessing? ' You will
get it by bringing in all the tithes, by giving yourself in
love and obedience and whole-hearted, joyous consecration to Jesus, as a true bride gives herself to her
husband. Do not try to bargain with the Lord and buy
it of Him, but wait on Him in never-give-in prayer and
confident expectation, and He will give it to you. Then
you must not hold it selfishly for your own gratification,
but let it overflow to the hungry, thirsty, fainting world

about you. God bless you even now, and do for you exceeding abundantly above all you ask or think!

A comrade went from one of my meetings recently with a heart greatly burdened for the blessing, and for two or three days and nights did little else but read the Bible and pray and cry to God for a clean heart filled with the Spirit. At last the Comforter came, and with Him fullness of peace and joy and soul-rest; and that day this comrade led a number of others into the blessing. Hallelujah! ' If ye then, being evil, know how to give good gifts unto your children: how much more shall your heavenly Father give the Holy Spirit to them that ask Him? ' (Luke xi. 13). ' *Ask . . . seek . . . knock.*'

' HAVE YE RECEIVED THE HOLY GHOST SINCE YE BELIEVED? '

CHAPTER XXII

Importance of the Doctrine and Experience of Holiness to Spiritual Leaders

' Ye shall receive power, after that the Holy Ghost is come upon you.'

A MIGHTY man inspires and trains other men to be mighty. We wonder and exclaim often at the slaughter of Goliath by David, and we forget that David was the forerunner of a race of fearless, invincible warriors and giant-killers.

If we would in this light but study and remember the story of David's mighty men, it would be most instructive to us.

Moses inspired a tribe of cowering, toiling, sweat-begrimed, spiritless slaves to lift up their heads, straighten their backs and throw off the yoke; and he led them forth with songs of victory and shouts of triumph from under the mailed hand and iron bondage of Pharaoh. He fired them with a national spirit, and welded and organized them into a distinct and compact people that could be hurled with resistless power against the walled cities and trained warriors of Canaan.

But what was the secret of David and Moses? Whence the superiority of these men? David was only a stripling shepherd-boy when he immortalized himself. What was his secret? To be sure, ' Moses was instructed in all the wisdom of the Egyptians ' (Acts vii. 22, R.V.), and, doubtless, had been trained in all the civil, military and scientific learning of his day; but he was so weak in himself that he feared and fled at the first word of questioning and disparagement that he heard (Exod. ii. 14), and spent the next forty years feeding sheep for another man in the rugged wilderness of Sinai. What, then, was his secret?

Doubtless, David and Moses were men cast in a kinglier mould than most men; but their secret was not in themselves.

Joseph Parker declared that great lives are built on great promises; and so they are. These men had so far humbled themselves that they found God. They got close to Him, and He spoke to them. He gave them promises. He revealed His way and truth to them and, trusting Him, believing His promises, and fashioning their lives according to His truth—His doctrine—everything else followed. They became 'workers together with God', heroes of faith, leaders of men, builders of empire, teachers of the race and, in an important sense, saviours of mankind.

Their secret is an open one; it is the secret of every truly successful spiritual leader from then till now, and there is no other way to success in spiritual leadership.

1. They had an *experience*. They *knew God*.

2. This experience, this acquaintance with God, was *maintained* and deepened and broadened in obedience to God's teaching, or truth, or doctrine.

3. They patiently yet urgently *taught others* what they themselves had learned, and declared, so far as they saw it, the whole counsel of God.

They were abreast of the deepest experiences and fullest revelations God had yet made to men. They were leaders, not laggards. They were not in the rear of the procession of God's warriors and saints; they were in the forefront.

Here we discover the importance of the doctrine and experience of holiness through the baptism of the Holy Spirit to Salvation Army leaders. We are to know God and glorify Him and reveal Him to men. We are to finish the work of Jesus, and 'fill up that which is behind of the afflictions of Christ' (Col. i. 24). We are to rescue the slaves of sin, to make a people, to fashion them into a holy nation, and inspire and lead them forth to save the world. How can we do this? Only by being in the forefront of God's spiritual hosts; not in name and in titles only, but in reality; by being in glad possession of the deepest experiences God gives and the fullest revelations He makes to men.

Our war is far more complex and desperate than that between nations and its issues are infinitely more far-reaching, and we must equip ourselves for it; and nothing is so vital to our cause as a mastery of the doctrine and an assured and joyous possession of the pentecostal experience of holiness through the indwelling Spirit.

I. *The Doctrine.*—What is the teaching of God's word about holiness?

1. If we carefully study God's word, we find that He wants His people to be holy, and the making of a holy people, after the pattern of Jesus, is the crowning work of the Holy Spirit. He commands us to ' cleanse ourselves from all filthiness of the flesh and spirit, perfecting holiness in the fear of God ' (2 Cor. vii. 1). It is prayed that we may ' increase and abound in love one toward another, and toward all men . . . To the end He may stablish your hearts unblameable in holiness before God ' (1 Thess. iii. 12, 13). He says: ' As He which hath called you is holy, so be ye holy in all manner of conversation; Because it is written, Be ye holy, for I am holy ' (1 Pet. i. 15, 16). And in the most earnest manner we are exhorted to ' follow peace with all men, and holiness, without which no man shall see the Lord ' (Heb. xii. 14).

2. As we further study the word, we discover that holiness is more than simple freedom from condemnation for wrong-doing. A helpless invalid lying on his bed of sickness, unable to do anything wrong, may be free from the condemnation of actual wrong-doing; yet it may be in his heart to do all manner of evil. Holiness on its negative side is a state of heart purity; it is heart cleanness—cleanness of thought and temper and disposition, cleanness of intention and purpose and wish; it is a state

of freedom from all sin, both inward and outward (Rom. vi. 18). On the positive side it is a state of union with God in Christ, in which the whole man becomes a temple of God and filled with the fruit of the Spirit, which is ' love, joy, peace, longsuffering, gentleness, goodness, faith, meekness, temperance ' (Gal. v. 22, 23). It is moral and spiritual sympathy and harmony with God in the holiness of His nature.

We must not, however, confound purity with maturity. Purity is a matter of the heart and is secured by an instantaneous act of the Holy Spirit; maturity is largely a matter of the head and results from growth in knowledge and experience. In one, the heart is made clean and is filled with love; in the other, the head is gradually corrected and filled with light, and so the heart is enlarged and more firmly established in faith; consequently, the experience deepens and becomes stronger and more robust in every way. It is for this reason that we need teachers after we are sanctified, and to this end we are exhorted to humbleness of mind.

With a heart full of sympathy and love for his father my little boy may voluntarily go into the garden to weed the vegetables; but, being yet ignorant, lacking light in his head, he pulls up my sweet corn with the grass and weeds. His little heart glows with pleasure and pride in the thought that he is ' helping papa '; yet he is doing the very thing I don't want him to do. But if I am a wise and patient father, I shall be pleased with him; for what is the loss of my few stalks of corn compared to the expression and development of his love and loyalty? And I shall commend him for the love and faithful purpose of his little heart, while I patiently set to work to enlighten the darkness of his little head. His heart is pure toward his father, but he is not yet mature. In this matter of light and maturity holy people often widely differ, and this causes much perplexity and needless and unwise anxiety. In the fourteenth chapter of Romans, Paul discusses and illustrates the principle underlying this distinction between purity and maturity.

3. As we continue to study the word under the illumination of the Spirit, who is given to lead us into all truth, we further learn that holiness is not a state which we reach in conversion. The apostles were converted, they had forsaken all to follow Jesus (Matt. xix. 27-29), their names were written in Heaven (Luke x. 20), and yet they were not holy. They doubted and feared, and again and again were they rebuked for the slowness and littleness of their faith. They were bigoted, and wanted to call down fire from Heaven to consume those who would not receive Jesus (Luke ix. 51-56); they were frequently contending among themselves as to which should be the greatest, and when the supreme test came they all forsook Him and fled. Certainly, they were not only afflicted with darkness in their heads, but, far worse, carnality in their hearts; they were His, and they were very dear to Him, but they were not yet holy, they were still impure of heart.

Paul makes this point very clear in his Epistle to the Corinthians. He tells them plainly that they were yet only babes in Christ, because they were carnal and contentious (1 Cor. iii. 1). They were in Christ, they had been converted, but they were not holy.

It is of great importance that we keep this truth well in mind that men may be truly converted, may be babes in Christ, and yet not be pure in heart; we shall then sympathize more fully with them, and see the more clearly how to help them and guide their feet into the way of holiness and peace.

Those who hold that we are sanctified wholly in conversion will meet with much to perplex them in their converts, and are not intelligently equipped to bless and help God's little children.

4. A continued study of God's teaching on this sub-ject will clearly reveal to us that purity of heart is obtained after we are converted. Peter makes this very plain in

his address to the Council in Jerusalem, where he recounts the outpouring of the Holy Spirit upon Cornelius and his household. After mentioning the gift of the Holy Ghost, he adds, ' and put no difference between us and them, purifying their hearts by faith ' (Acts xv. 9). Among other things, then, the baptism of the Holy Ghost purifies the heart; but the disciples were converted before they received this pentecostal experience, so we see that heart purity, or holiness, is a work wrought in us after conversion.

Again, we notice that Peter says, ' purifying their hearts by faith '. If it is by faith, then it is not by growth, nor by works, nor by death, nor by purgatory after death. It is God's work. He purifies the heart, and He does it for those, and only those, who, devoting all their possessions and powers to Him, seek Him by simple, prayerful, obedient, expectant, unwavering faith through His Son our Saviour.

Unless we grasp these truths and hold them firmly, we shall not be able rightly to divide the word of truth, we shall hardly be workmen that need not be ashamed, approved unto God (2 Tim. ii. 15). Someone has written that ' the searcher in science knows that if he but stumble in his hypothesis—that if he but let himself be betrayed into prejudice or undue leaning toward a pet theory, or anything but absolute uprightness of mind—his whole work will be stultified and he will fail ignominiously. To get anywhere in science he must follow truth with absolute rectitude '.

And is there not a science of salvation, holiness, eternal life, that requires the same absolute loyalty to ' the Spirit of truth '? How infinitely important, then, that we know what that truth is, that we may understand and hold that doctrine.

A friend of mine who finished his course with joy and was called into the presence of his Lord to receive his crown some time ago, has pointed out some mistakes which we must carefully avoid:

It is a great mistake to substitute repentance for Bible consecration. The people whom Paul exhorted to full sanctification were those who had turned from their idols to serve the living and true God, and to wait for His Son sent down from Heaven (1 Thess. i. 9, 10; iii. 10-13; v. 23).

Only people who are citizens of His kingdom can claim His sanctifying power. Those who still have idols to renounce may be candidates for conversion, but not for the baptism with the Holy Ghost and fire.

It is a mistake in consecration to suppose that the person making it has anything of his own to give. We are not our own, but we are bought with a price, and consecration is simply taking our hands off from God's property. To withhold wilfully anything from God is to be a God-robber.

It is a mistake to substitute a mere mental assent to God's proprietorship and right to all we have, while withholding complete devotion to Him. This is theoretical consecration—a rock on which we fear multitudes are being wrecked. Consecration which does not embrace the crucifixion of self and the funeral of all false ambitions is not the kind which will bring the holy fire. A consecration is imperfect which does not embrace the speaking faculty (the tongue), the believing faculty (the heart), the imagination, and every power of mind, soul and body, giving all absolutely and for ever into the hands of Jesus and turning a deaf ear to every opposing voice.

Have you made such a consecration as this? It must embrace all this, or it will prove a bed of quicksand to sink your soul, instead of a full salvation balloon, which will safely bear you above the fog, malaria and turmoil of the world. There you can triumphantly sing:

> I rise to float in realms of light
>   Above the world and sin,
> With heart made pure and garments white,
>   And Christ enthroned within.

It is a mistake to teach seekers to ' only believe ', without complete abandonment to God at every point, for they can no more do it than an anchored ship can sail.

It is a mistake to substitute mere verbal assent for obedient trust. ' Only believe ' is a fatal snare to all who fall into these traps.

It is a mistake to believe that the altar sanctifies the gift without the assurance that all is on the altar. If even the end of your tongue, one cent of your money, or a straw's weight of false ambition or spirit of dictation, or one ounce of your reputation, will or believing powers be left off the altar, you can no more believe than a bird without wings can fly.

' Only believe ' is only for those seekers of holiness who are truly converted, fully consecrated, and crucified to everything but the whole will of God. Teachers who apply this to people who have not yet reached these stations need themselves to be taught. All who have reached them may believe and, if they do believe, may look God in the face and triumphantly sing:

> The Blood, the Blood is all my plea,
> Hallelujah, for it cleanseth me.

II. *The Experience.*—Simply to be skilled in the doctrine is not sufficient for us as leaders. We may be as orthodox as St. Paul himself, and yet be only as ' sounding brass, or a clanging cymbal ', unless we are rooted in the blessed experience of holiness. If we would save ourselves and them that follow us, if we would make havoc of the devil's kingdom and build up God's kingdom, we must not only know and preach the truth, but we must be living examples of the saving and sanctifying power of the truth. We are to be living epistles, ' known and read of all men ' (2 Cor. iii. 2); we must be able to say with Paul, ' Be ye followers of me, even as I also am of Christ ' (1 Cor. xi. 1), and ' those things, which ye have both learned, and received, and heard, and seen in me, do: and the God of peace shall be with you ' (Phil. iv. 9).

We must not forget that:

1. We are ourselves simple Christians, individual souls struggling for eternal life and liberty; we must by all means save ourselves. To this end we must be holy, else we shall at last experience the awful woe of those who, having preached to others, are yet themselves castaways.

2. We are leaders upon whom multitudes depend. It is a joy and an honour to be a leader, but it is also a grave responsibility. James says: ' We shall receive heavier judgement ' (Jas. iii. 1, R.V.). How unspeakable shall be our blessedness and how vast our reward, if, wise in the doctrine, rich, strong and clean in the experience of holiness, we lead our people into their full

heritage in Jesus! But how terrible shall be our condemnation, how great our loss, if, in spiritual sloth-
fulness and unbelief, we stop short of the experience
ourselves and leave them to perish for want of the
gushing waters, heavenly food and divine direction we
should have brought them! We need the experience for
ourselves, and we need it for our work and our people.

What the roof is to a house, doctrine is to our system
of truth. It completes it. What sound and robust
health is to our bodies, experience is to our souls. It
makes us every whit whole and fits us for all duty.
Sweep away the doctrine and the experience will soon
be lost. Lose the experience and the doctrine will surely
be neglected, if not attacked and denied. No man can
have the heart, even if he has the head, to preach the
doctrine fully, faithfully and constantly unless he has
the experience.

Spiritual things are spiritually discerned, and as this
doctrine deals with the deepest things of the Spirit, it is
only clearly understood and best recommended,
explained, defended and enforced by those who have
the experience.

Without the experience, the presentation of the
doctrine will be faulty, cold and lifeless, or weak and
vacillating, or harsh, sharp and severe. With the
experience, the preaching of the doctrine will be with
great joy and assurance; it will be strong and searching,
but at the same time warm, persuasive and tender.

I shall never forget the shock of mingled surprise,
amusement and grief with which I heard a Captain
loudly announce in one of my meetings many years ago
that he was ' going to preach holiness now '. His people
would ' have to get it ', if he had to ' ram it down their
throats '. Poor fellow! He did not possess the experience
himself; he never pressed into it, and soon forsook his
people.

A man in the clear experience of the blessing will
never think of ' ramming ' it down people; but will,

with much secret prayer, constant meditation and study, patient instruction, faithful warning, loving persuasion, and burning, joyful testimony, seek to lead them into that entire and glad consecration, that fullness of faith, that never fails to receive the blessing.

Again, the most accurate and complete knowledge of the doctrine and the fullest possession of the experience, will fail us at last unless we carefully guard ourselves at several points and watch and pray.

3. We must not judge ourselves so much by our feelings as by our volitions. It is not my feelings, but the purpose of my heart, the attitude of my will, that God looks at, and it is that to which I must look. ' If our heart condemn us not, then have we confidence toward God ' (1 John iii. 21). A friend of mine who had firmly grasped this thought and walked continually with God used to testify: ' I am just as good when I don't feel good as when I do feel good.' Another mighty man of God said that all the feeling he needed to enable him to trust God was the consciousness that he was fully submitted to all the known will of God.

We must not forget that the devil is ' the accuser of our brethren ' (Rev. xii. 10), and that he seeks to turn our eyes away from Jesus, who is our Surety and our Advocate, to ourselves, our feelings, infirmities, and failures. If he succeeds in this, gloom will fill us, doubts and fears will spring up within us and we shall soon fail and fall. We must be wise as the conies; we must build our nest in the cleft of the Rock of ages. Hallelujah!

4. We must not divorce conduct from character, or works from faith. Our lives must square with our teaching. We must live what we preach. We must not suppose that faith in Jesus excuses us from patient, faithful, laborious service. We must live ' by every word that proceedeth out of the mouth of God ' (Matt. iv. 4); that is, we must fashion our lives, conduct, conversation by the principles laid down in His word, remembering His searching saying, ' Not every one

that saith unto Me, Lord, Lord, shall enter into the Kingdom of Heaven; but he that doeth the will of My Father which is in Heaven ' (Matt. vii. 21).

This subject of faith and works is very fully discussed by James (ii. 14-26). Paul is very clear in his teaching that, while God saves us not by our works but by His mercy through faith, ' we are His workmanship, created in Christ Jesus unto good works, which God hath before ordained that we should walk in them ' (Eph. ii. 8-10).

Faith must ' work by love ', emotion must be transmitted into action, joy must lead to work, and love to faithful, self-sacrificing service, else they become a kind of pleasant and respectable, but none the less deadly, debauchery.

5. However blessed and satisfactory our present experience may be, we must not rest in it; we must remember that our Lord has yet many things to say unto us, as we are able to receive them. We must stir up the gift of God that is in us, and say with Paul: ' One thing I do, forgetting the things which are behind, and stretching forward (as a racer) to the things which are before, I press on toward the goal unto the prize of the high calling of God in Christ Jesus ' (Phil. iii. 13, 14, R.V.). It is at this point that many fail. They seek the Lord, they weep, struggle, pray, and then they believe; but, instead of pressing on, they sit down to enjoy the blessing and, lo! is it not. The children of Israel must needs follow the pillar of cloud and fire. It made no difference when it moved—by day or by night, they followed; and when the Comforter comes we must follow, if we would abide in Him and be filled with all the fullness of God. And, Oh, the joy of following Him!

Finally, if we have the blessing—not the harsh, narrow, unprogressive exclusiveness which often calls itself by the sweet, heavenly term of holiness, but the vigorous, courageous, self-sacrificing, tender, pentecostal experience of perfect love—we shall both save ourselves and enlighten the world; our converts will be strong, our candidates for the work will multiply and be able, dare-devil men and women, and our people will come to be like the brethren of Gideon, who ' resembled the children of a king ' (Judges viii. 18).

' HAVE YE RECEIVED THE HOLY GHOST SINCE YE BELIEVED ? '

CHAPTER XXIII

Victory over Evil Temper by the Power of the Holy Spirit

' Ye shall receive power, after that the Holy Ghost is come upon you.'

TWO letters recently reached me, one from Oregon and one from Massachusetts, inquiring if I thought it possible to have temper destroyed. The comrade from Oregon wrote: ' I have been wondering if the statement is correct when one says, " My temper is all taken away." Do you think the temper is destroyed or sanctified? It seems to me that if one's temper were actually gone one would not be good for anything.'

The comrade from Massachusetts wrote: ' Two of our corps cadets have had the question put to them, " Is it possible to have all temper taken out of our hearts? " One claims it is possible. The other holds that the temper is not taken out, but God gives power to overcome it.'

Evidently these are questions that perplex many people, and yet the answer seems to me simple.

Temper, in the sense the word is generally used, is not a faculty or power of the soul, but rather an irregular, passionate, violent expression of selfishness. When selfishness is destroyed by love, by the incoming of the Holy Spirit, revealing Jesus to us as an uttermost Saviour and creating within us a clean heart, such evil temper is gone, just as the friction and consequent wear and heat of two wheels is gone when the cogs are perfectly adjusted to each other. As wheels are far better off without friction, so man is far better off without such temper.

149

We do not destroy the wheels to get rid of the friction, but we readjust them; we put them into just or right relations to each other, then noiselessly and perfectly they do their work. So, strictly speaking, sanctification does not destroy self, but selfishness—the abnormal, mean and disordered manifestation and assertion of self. I myself am to be sanctified, rectified, purified, brought into harmony with God's will as revealed in His word, and united to Him in Jesus, so that His life of holiness and love flows continually through all the avenues of my being, as the sap of the vine flows through all parts of the branch. ' I am the vine, ye are the branches,' said Jesus (John xv. 5).

When a man is thus filled with the Holy Spirit he is not made into a putty man, a jelly fish, with all powers of resistance taken out of him; he does not have any less ' push ' and ' go ' than before, but rather more, for all his natural energy is now reinforced by the Holy Spirit and turned into channels of love and peace instead of hate and strife.

He may still feel indignation in the presence of wrong, but it will no longer be rash, violent, explosive and selfish, but calm and orderly, holy, determined, like that of God. It will be the wholesome, natural antagonism of holiness and righteousness to all unrighteousness and evil.

Such a man will feel it when he is wronged, but it will be much in the same way that he feels when others are wronged. The personal, selfish element will be absent. At the same time there will be compassion for the wrong-doer and a greater desire to see him saved than to see him punished.

A sanctified man was walking down the street the other day with his wife, when a filthy fellow on a passing wagon insulted her with foul words. Instantly the temptation came to the man to want to get hold of him and punish him, but as instantly the indwelling Comforter whispered, ' If ye will forgive men their trespasses.'

Instantly the clean heart of the man responded, 'I will, I do forgive him, Lord.'   Then instead of anger a great love filled his soul, instead of hurling a brick or hot words at the poor devil-deceived sinner, he sent a prayer to God in Heaven for him.   There was no friction in his soul.   He was perfectly adjusted to his Lord; his heart was perfectly responsive to his Master's word, and he could rightly say, ' My temper is gone.'

A man must have his spiritual eyes wide open to discern the difference between sinful temper and righteous indignation.

Many a man wrongs and robs himself by calling his fits of temper ' righteous indignation'; while, on the other hand, there are timid souls who are so afraid of sinning through temper that they suppress the wholesome antagonism that righteousness, to be healthy and perfect, must express toward all unrighteousness and sin.

It takes the keen-edged word of God, applied by the Holy Spirit, to cut away unholy temper without destroying righteous antagonism; to enable a man to hate and fight sin with spiritual weapons (2 Cor. x. 3-5), while pitying and loving the sinner; so to fill him with the mind of Jesus that he will feel as badly over a wrong done to a stranger as though it were done to himself; to help him to put away the personal feeling and be as calm, unselfish and judicial in opposing wrong as is the judge upon the bench.   Into this state of heart and mind is one brought who is entirely sanctified by the indwelling Holy Spirit.   Hallelujah!

Dr. Asa Mahan, the friend and co-worker of Finney, had a quick and violent temper in his youth and young manhood; but one day he believed and God sanctified him, and for fifty years he said he never felt more than one uprising of temper, and that was but for an instant, about five years after he received the blessing.   For the following forty-five years, though subjected to many trials and provocations, he felt only love, peace, patience and goodwill in his heart.

A Christian woman was confined to her bed for years and was very touchy and petulant. At last she became convinced that the Lord had a better experience for her, and she began to pray for a clean heart full of patient, holy, humble love. She prayed so earnestly and violently that her family became alarmed lest she should wear her poor, frail body out in her struggle for spiritual freedom. But she told them she was determined to have the blessing if it cost her her life. She continued to pray until one glad, sweet day the Comforter came; her heart was purified. From that day forth, despite her remaining a nervous invalid, suffering constant pain, she never showed the least sign of temper or impatience; instead she was full of meekness and patient, joyous thankfulness.

> Love took up the harp of life, and smote on all the chords with might—
> Smote the chord of self that, trembling, passed in music out of sight.

Such is the experience of one in whom Jesus lives without a rival, and in whom grace has wrought its perfect work.

' No form of vice, not worldliness, not greed of gold, not drunkenness itself, does more to un-Christianize society than evil temper,' says a distinguished and thoughtful writer.

If this be true, it must be God's will that we be saved from it. And it is provided for in the uttermost salvation that Jesus offers.

Do you want this blessing, my brother, my sister? If so, be sure of this, God has not begotten such a desire in your heart to mock you; you may have it. God is able to do even this for you. With man it is impossible, but not with God. Look at Him just now for it. It is His work, His gift. Look at your past failures and acknowledge them; look at your present and future difficulties, count them up and face them every one, and admit that they are more than you can hope to conquer. Then look at the dying Son of God, your Saviour—the Man with the seamless robe, the crown of thorns, and the nail-prints; look at the fountain of His Blood; look at His word; look at the almighty Holy Ghost, who will dwell within you if you but trust and obey. Cry out: ' It shall be done! The mountain shall become a plain; the impossible shall become possible. Hallelujah! ' Quietly, intelligently, abandon yourself to the Holy Spirit just now in simple, glad, obedient faith, and the blessing shall be yours. Glory to God!

' HAVE YE RECEIVED THE HOLY GHOST SINCE YE BELIEVED? '